Simple Upholstery & Slipcovers

Simple Upholstery & Slipcovers

Great New Looks for Every Room

CAROL PARKS

Sterling Publishing Co., Inc. New York
A Sterling/Lark Book

Art and Production: Elaine Thompson
Photography: Evan Bracken, Light Reflections; and Ariadne/Spaarnestad
Illustrations: Kay Holmes Stafford
Editorial assistance: Val Anderson

Library of Congress Cataloging-in-Publication Data
Parks, Carol
    Simple upholstery & slipcovers : great new looks for every room /
Carol Parks.
       p.   cm.
    "A Sterling/Lark book."
    Includes index.
    ISBN 0-8069-8158-X
    1. Slip covers.   2. Upholstery.   3. Cushions.   I. Title.
TT395.P37   1996
    746.9'5--dc20   96-24162
                                                         CIP

10 9 8 7 6 5 4 3 2 1

A Sterling/Lark Book

First paperback edition published in 1997 by
    Sterling Publishing Company, Inc.
    387 Park Avenue South, New York, N.Y. 10016

Created and produced by Altamont Press, Inc.
    50 College Street, Asheville, NC 28801

© 1996 by Altamont Press

Distributed in Canada by Sterling Publishing
    c/o Canadian Manda Group, One Atlantic Avenue, Suite 105, Toronto, Ontario,
    Canada M6K 3E7

Distributed in Great Britain and Europe by Cassell PLC
    Wellington House, 125 Strand, London WC2R 0BB, England

Distributed in Australia by Capricorn Link (Australia) Pty Ltd.
    P.O. Box 6651, Baulkham Hills, Business Centre, NSW 2153, Australia

Sterling ISBN 0-8069-8158-X Trade
            0-8069-8159-8 Paper

Acknowledgements

*Several people deserve hearty thanks for their contributions to this book.
We are grateful to them for sharing their time and their expertise.*

◈

Louise Sheaffer, *artful slipcover-maker, graciously allowed us to photograph her at work as she rejuvenated the model couch and chair shown in Chapter 5.*

Hugh Redwood, *master upholsterer, patient educator, and entertaining storyteller, was a most genial host during our photographic invasion of his workplace.*

Dana Irwin *and* **Susan Kieffer** *exhibited great faith in offering up their treasured pieces of furniture for rehabilitation in front of the camera.*

The people at **Swatches** *invited us to sample their wonderful collection of fabrics and trims for photography.*

Lucile Neilson *generously shared with us a great bound buttonhole technique learned from her mother, Olive B. Roberts. It is illustrated on page 77.*

And special thanks always to the talented people who provided the pictures.
Kay Holmes Stafford *rendered the line illustrations throughout the book.*
Evan Bracken *took the photographs that appear on the following pages:
10–23, 28, 52–69, 104–124, 143, and the endpapers.*

Contents

Introduction 9

1 · Materials 11

2 · Tools and Equipment 21

3 · Cushions and Pillows 25

4 · Simple Cover-Ups 33

5 · Making a Tailored Slipcover 53

6 · Tailored Slipcover Projects 73

7 · Quick Upholstery 91

8 · Reupholstering a Chair 105

9 · Upholstery Projects 127

Index 141

Introduction

New dressing for the furniture can alter the look of a room more effectively than any other change you can make. Even the simplest cover for an ottoman—a bright fabric square knotted at the corners—can perk up a dreary decor in an instant. With a reupholstering job that includes the couch and easy chairs, the room can be given a brand new style or color scheme.

Slipcovers, in general, are those removable loose covers that can be replaced fairly quickly when a change is called for. In its most basic form, a slipcover might be just a length of fabric, artfully draped and tied in place. With the investment of just a little more time, a few quick seams can be used to shape the cover to the contours of the chair. A very fitted, well-tailored slipcover, trimmed with welt and complemented with matching cushion covers, takes on the look of upholstery but still can be removed for laundering or cleaning.

Upholstery is more permanent by nature. Fabric is attached directly to the furniture frame over some degree of padding. Except for making welt and stitching the occasional dart, there is almost no sewing involved.

Reupholstery projects, too, vary in complexity and time requirements. Replacing the fabric cover on a chair seat that is in good condition can take an hour from start to finish. A thorough reupholstering job that includes stripping a chair to the frame and replacing the padding before applying a new cover will take considerably longer—and will result in a better-than-brand-new piece of furniture.

The photos in the following chapters illustrate a range of designs, from the quickest and simplest imaginable to traditional, tailored slipcovers and upholstery. Whether you plan to make a slipcover or to reupholster, look at all the designs for the other technique too; there are many features that can be applied with great success to either upholstery or slipcovers.

If your slipcover-making experience is limited, or if you have never tried upholstery, follow the illustrated step-by-step instructions to learn how the pros work. Even if the chair or couch you are renovating does not match our model, the techniques will be the same or nearly so. You'll find thorough instructions, too, for installing a slipcover zipper, for making and applying welt, and for constructing cushions in several different styles.

One of the most gratifying of decorating moments comes when you finally zip a just-completed slipcover over your favorite chair, or plump up the cushions on a newly reupholstered couch. Then you can stand back for an admiring look at what you have accomplished. And you need not tell anyone that the most difficult part of the job was choosing the fabric!

1 • Materials

*T*he fabric you choose for upholstery or slipcovers, more than any other element, will determine whether the project is pleasurable or frustrating. Find the perfect color, of course, but also give consideration to the fabric's fiber content, weave structure, and pattern.

THE FIBERS OF FABRICS

The fiber is the raw material from which a fabric is made, such as cotton, wool, silk, polyester, nylon, and so on. The fiber content determines how a fabric should be handled during construction, whether it will wash well—or at all, whether it will wrinkle terribly, whether it will fade in sunlight, and how durable the resulting article will be. Fabrics can be made of either natural fibers or synthetic fibers, or are blends of the two.

NATURAL FIBER FABRICS

Cotton, linen, and ramie are the most popular of the natural fibers that originate from plants. Wool and silk, animal fibers, come from the backs of sheep and from the cocoons of silkworms, respectively. Natural fiber fabrics have the aesthetic qualities that synthetics strive to replicate. In general, these fabrics are more comfortable to use because they "breathe," allowing air to circulate and moisture to evaporate away. Generally speaking, natural fiber fabrics are easier to work with than synthetics; they can easily be sewn or pressed into shape. Many natural fiber fabrics, however, have a tendency to wrinkle.

Cotton fabrics are perhaps the best all around for decorating. Depending upon the weave and the surface texture, cottons are easy to sew and to shape. Most can be laundered. Many are very durable. Although some cotton fabrics resist wrinkling, a synthetic such as polyester is often blended with the cotton fiber to produce this quality, resulting in a fabric that is a bit more difficult to ease into shape during construction, but that maintains a neat appearance in the finished article.

Linen is the most durable natural fiber fabric. It stands up well to repeated laundering, and—to some eyes—becomes more beautiful with age. Linen does wrinkle. Depending upon your point of view, that characteristic can be part of its charm. After much washing and wear, though, its wrinkles take the form of genteel rumpling rather than sharp creases. Linen is often combined with other fibers to produce a fabric that is more crease resistant or less costly.

There is an unfortunate trend among bargain fabric stores to label as "linen" inferior synthetic blend fabrics that have a surface texture and weave similar to linen. Check the bolt carefully to be sure the fiber content is linen. These imitations do not have the qualities or the strength of the real thing.

Ramie, a plant fiber, produces a fabric similar in appearance to linen. It is not quite as durable, nor is it as expensive. It is frequently blended with linen as a good compromise.

Silk fibers also produce fabrics with a distinctive appearance. Silk fabrics generally are not as durable as cotton or linen, but can make beautiful coverings for furnishings that are not subjected to heavy use. While silk has a reputation for being expensive, many silk fabrics are no more costly than good quality cotton.

Tussah, or raw silk, is in the moderate price range and has a wonderfully nubby texture that works well with informal furnishings.

Silk noil is quite inexpensive, washes nicely (although it must be preshrunk), and has a good draping quality that is well suited to loose-fitting slipcovers and the like.

MAN-MADE FIBERS

Synthetic fibers, such as nylon and polyester, are often blended with natural fibers to add durability and wrinkle resistance, and to produce fabrics that are lower in cost. Such blends can be more stable and easier to care for than the natural fiber counterparts. Most moderately priced fabrics available to the home upholsterer are blends of this sort, and work well for many projects.

Fabrics made entirely of synthetic fiber are not as good a choice. They can be slippery. They won't mold as well to the shape of the furniture. They are uncomfortable, especially in hot and humid climates.

Commercially upholstered furniture often is covered with all-synthetic fabric in the interest of economy and durability. Mill end and outlet stores often carry a large assortment of these fabrics. They can be very strong and sturdy, but not a good bet for the amateur upholsterer. Few home sewing machines can manage these tough fabrics. The coating often applied to the wrong side for added stability causes further difficulty with a non-industrial machine.

When buying a fabric blend, be aware of the qualities of the fibers that make it up. The following are synthetics often used with natural fibers in decorating fabrics.

Acrylic fiber adds a wear-resistant quality to velvets and plushes. It has little fabric "memory," however, and does not regain its shape once it is stretched. It is resistant to sun fading.

Nylon is extremely durable. It is short of aesthetic appeal, but adds strength and durability to other fibers. All-nylon upholstery fabrics, often used commercially, are very difficult for a home machine to manage.

Polyester is the synthetic most commonly used in decorating fabrics. It is strong, it dyes well, and it resists sun fading. Like other synthetics, it has poor memory. It is often blended with cotton, wool, and linen to add wrinkle resistance to those fibers.

Polypropylene fibers, like nylon, are extremely strong and durable, but do not have nylon's resistance to sunlight. They are very inexpensive to produce and so are often used to upholster lower priced furniture. An industrial machine is essential for sewing them.

Rayon is somewhat of a hybrid; it is a man-made fiber that originates from cellulose, a natural material. It does not wear well, but has an attractive draping quality and sheen. It is relatively inexpensive. It is often blended with other fabrics, imparting its own characteristics to the resulting fabric. Most rayons and rayon blends should be dry cleaned.

WEAVES AND SURFACE PATTERNS

Some fabrics are known best by the surface patterning or the weave than by the fiber content. Velvet, for example, refers to the smooth pile surface of the fabric. Velvet can be made of several different fibers and combinations—silk, wool, cotton (also known as "velveteen"), and blends of these fibers with synthetics. "Brocade" refers to a pattern woven into the cloth, sometimes in several colors. Brocades, too, can be manufactured of any number of different fibers.

Sateen is fabric with a built-in surface sheen. The term usually refers to cotton or cotton blend with a satin weave structure. Sateen retains its sheen through wear and laundering because it is woven into the cloth. Cotton chintz, or polished cotton, is similar in appearance but derives its sheen from a chemical finishing process. The first laundering or several trips to the dry cleaner will dull the finish. It wears off with use, too.

While the weave or surface texture affects to some degree the way a chosen fabric will handle during construction, its durability, and its care requirements, the fiber content is more important in these instances. There is polyester and cotton velvet, for example, that responds beautifully to machine washing and drying. Silk velvet would be ruined by such treatment.

DECORATOR FABRICS vs. FASHION FABRICS

Materials manufactured especially for use in home decorating—upholstery, slipcovers, or window treatments—differ in several respects from fabrics intended for clothing construction. Decorating fabrics are generally woven in 54-inch (137-cm) widths, while fashion fabrics are most often 45 inches (115 cm) wide. This seemingly small difference can be important in slipcover or upholstery projects. Narrower fabric can necessitate tedious and difficult piecing and pattern matching.

Decorator fabrics, particularly cottons, are often treated with special finishes to render them resistant to creasing and soiling, and to add stability to the fabric. This, in part, accounts for their relatively higher prices. There is a difference in the prints and patterns, too. Decorator fabrics often feature bold prints with large repeats and strong color combinations that most people would not choose to wear.

Some decorator fabrics are manufactured with railroading in mind; that is, the pattern is woven or printed across the fabric instead of being oriented lengthwise. These fabrics are usually quite stable on the crossgrain too. "Railroading" means using the fabric in upholstery or slipcovers with the lengthwise grain running horizontally along the piece of furniture rather than in the normal vertical direction. When the covering is for a couch, railroading can save considerable fabric and reduce the number of seams required.

TRIMS

Shops that sell decorator fabrics will usually have an assortment of gimp, braids, welt cord, and fringe in colors to coordinate with fabric lines. These offer plenty of design potential. Most are made in a blend of rayon and cotton, meaning they are not washable.

FABRIC GRAIN

The grain of the fabric—the direction of the threads that make up its weave—affects the behavior and handling of a piece of cloth. Slipcovers and upholstery, just like articles of clothing, usually are cut with the lengthwise fabric grain along the vertical lines of the chair (or person) for which they are made. The lengthwise grain of the fabric, parallel to the finished selvage edges, usually is strongest and stretches least.

The crossgrain is parallel to the cut or torn edges. Most woven fabrics stretch slightly more in this direction than they do along the lengthwise grain.

The fabric's true bias is at a 45-degree angle to the lengthwise and crosswise grainlines. There is usually considerable stretch along a fabric's bias.

Designs for upholstery and slipcovers, as for clothing, make use of the different fabric grains to accomplish different effects. Vertical sections are cut on the lengthwise grain so they will not hang out of shape. The crossgrain, then, goes around the chair, or body, to conform to curves more often found in that direction.

Often the bias grain, by default or design, ends up at points where extra flexibility is needed. On a shirt or dress, the curve of an underarm seam is on the bias. On a wing chair, the seam at the base of the wing is often cut with a bias orientation. Welt trim is cut on the bias so it will conform neatly to curved seams and corners.

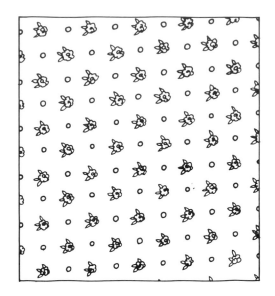

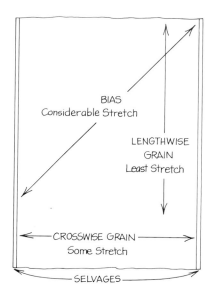

OFF-GRAIN PATTERNS

Because of the way patterns are printed onto fabric, a visibly horizontal pattern can end up out of line with the fabric's grain. When fabric is cut on the grain, the pattern appears crooked. Prints like these should not be used for slipcover or upholstery projects where large areas of fabric are visible.

Be wary, too, of stripes and checks that are printed on rather than woven into the fabric. When printed off grain, as they often are, the article made from such a fabric will appear skewed.

SLIPCOVER AND UPHOLSTERY FABRICS

An advantage to slipcovers is that almost any fabric can be used to make them. Tailored, fitted covers call for a medium or heavier weight cloth with good stability, but there are slipcover designs shown throughout these chapters to accommodate fabrics of every description. Let the style of the cover guide your choice.

Do avoid the heavy upholstery fabrics when making slipcovers. They are best used just for upholstery.

Take into consideration the intended life of the cover and where it will be used. Is the fabric sturdy enough to last for several years in the family room, or will it cover a primarily decorative bedroom chair? How much care are you willing to provide? You may not really want a sparkling white cover on the most comfortable living room chair if you have several teenagers in residence.

Consider, too, the formal or casual nature of the fabric against the furniture it will adorn. A delicate Chippendale chair might look better in silk shantung than denim, which would be more appropriate for the lumpy couch in the TV room than would the silk.

Upholstery fabric should be of moderate to heavy weight and very stable. Choose a durable fabric that will last until you tire of it.

Many fabrics that are not manufactured with upholstery in mind will work beautifully, and will perhaps produce unexpected and exciting results. Check carefully to be sure the fabric has the necessary qualities, then enjoy some experimentation.

Upholstery fabrics, like those for slipcovers, should meet your standards for care (or lack of it) and compatibility with the furniture. Your standards might be somewhat higher for upholstery since it should not need to be replaced as soon as a slipcover might.

PREPARING FABRICS

Upholstery fabric requires no preliminary work before you cut into it. Fabrics for a slipcover, however, should be preshrunk if you will wash the cover.

Preshrinking is simply a matter of washing and drying the fabric by the same method you will use with the finished article. Then press the fabric, always with the lengthwise grain, before you cut. As added insurance, preshrink all materials that will go into the cover: welt cord, the zipper, and any trim.

MATERIALS JUST FOR UPHOLSTERY

An upholstery project will require some specialized and unfamiliar materials that are used under, or to attach, the covering. If there is no upholstery supplier in your area, check with a shop that sells decorator fabrics.

Cambric, *bottom cloth*, or *dust cover* are several terms used for the final covering used to neaten the underside of a chair or couch and keep out the dust. Originally tightly woven, dustproof cotton cambric fabric was used for this purpose and still is a good choice. Upholsterers now use a nonwoven synthetic material made for the purpose and less expensive. It is affixed with the shiny side out.

Platform cloth is another upholsterer's specialty fabric. It is used for the out-of-sight platform, or deck, section of a chair or couch that is usually attached to the front panel of the upholstery or slipcover. The fabric is inexpensive; a strong, lightweight synthetic with little stretch in either direction. Any fabric with these characteristics would work just as well.

Upholstery materials, clockwise from lower right: dust cover cloth, webbing, edge rolls, platform cloth, welt cord, polyester batting, cotton felt.

Essential upholsterer's supplies, clockwise from lower right: tacking strips, tack strips, flexible metal tack strip, decorative tacks, spring tying cord, zipper, assorted threads.

Padding and Stuffing

Most upholstered furniture utilizes a combination of materials. A seat cushion may contain dense foam. Cotton batting is used where firm padding is needed, with polyester batting for resiliency and for areas that require shaping.

Fillings and foams for cushions are described in more detail on page 25. For drop-in seats, like those of many dining chairs, **curled hair** and **coir fiber** are good alternatives to foam. Before state-of-the-art foam seat cushions were available, these fibers were used almost exclusively and they are still used regularly in restoration work. The material

can be shaped, and it offers firm support with some give. On the down side, it tends to bottom out eventually.

Cotton batting, or **felt**, provides a soft, dense, and somewhat resilient first layer of padding. It can be used exclusively on a piece, too, if a great deal of springiness is not desired. It is available in rolls.

Polyester batting also is a stock item with upholstery suppliers and is available in rolls. It is lightweight and springy, and it is slower to compress than cotton.

Support Materials

Webbing, traditionally made of jute, provides a base for seat springs in chairs that have them, or the seat padding of straight chairs. Webbing sags after a time, and the start of a reupholstery job offers the ideal opportunity to replace it. The companion tool, the **webbing stretcher**, is nearly essential but reasonably priced.

Spring tying cord holds coil springs together and controls the contour shaped by their upper rings.

Threads for upholstery work are heavier than standard sewing thread. Fabrics often are quite thick and strong, and seams must withstand considerable strain.

Zippers allow cushion covers to be removed for cleaning. A zipper is often the closure of choice at one or both back corners of a slipcover. Heavy-duty zippers can be purchased by the inch or by the roll from upholstery suppliers. Cut ends are easily secured by a few stitches with the above-mentioned heavy thread.

Attaching the Fabric

The materials described below are used for the upholstery projects in Chapters 8 and 9. Many other specialty aids are manufactured for particular upholstering situations and styles. If your project presents an unusual problem, there is bound to be a solution available.

Upholstery tacks today are used far less frequently than staples. They may be the choice for an authentic restoration job or if the project is too small to warrant the purchase of a heavy-duty stapler. They are sold in a sterile condition. The most convenient place to keep them while working is in the mouth.

Decorative tacks come in several sizes and finishes. They are meant to be seen, and are often used in conjunction with decorative braids.

Tack strip is available in pre-cut lengths. Tack heads are embedded in firm cardboard, ready to attach.

Tacking strip—fiber strips without the tacks—is used where it can be stapled invisibly under a fabric layer, generally along a straight edge. It is sold in rolls.

Flexible metal tack strip, with tacks built in, provides a clever means of attaching a folded fabric edge neatly around curves and corners.

WELT

Cord that is covered with fabric and sewn into a seam is "piping" when it is applied to clothing and more often "welt" when it embellishes furniture or home accessories. Whatever you choose to call it, welt provides a professional-looking finish to seat cushions and pillows and to seams and edges of slipcovers and upholstered pieces.

Welting serves several practical purposes, too. In furniture coverings, it strengthens seams with an additional line of stitching. It acts as a buffer against untimely wear along edges and at corners. In upholstery, it covers the lines where two fabric panels meet. On cushions and slipcovers it can even up less than perfect seamlines. Bias-cut welting in the seams of checked or striped fabrics provides a pleasant visual diversion and distracts the eye from seams in which the pattern cannot be matched perfectly.

Self welting is most often the choice for traditional slipcovers and upholstery. It is easily made by stitching a fabric strip around a length of purchased cord. Polyester piping or welt cord is available in diameters ranging from about $\frac{1}{8}$ inch (3 mm) to an inch (2.5 cm) or more. Thicker cord exaggerates the seamlines to provide a bold accent for a large pil-

low or squatty footstool. Very fine cord adds a more subtle finish, appropriate for a delicate chair, for example. For most furniture coverings, cord $\frac{1}{4}$ to $\frac{3}{8}$ inch (.5 to 1 cm) in diameter is standard.

Welting on a cushion or upholstered chair offers a grand opportunity for creative expression. It's fun to try a contrasting color or a complementary pattern. Fabric of the same color but with a different texture or weave can add interest to the piece.

Manufactured welt is another option. It is available in a wide range of colors and sizes from interior designers and where decorator fabrics are sold. Some fabric manufacturers make welt in colors to match their top-of-the-line patterns. Most purchased welt should be dry cleaned, so should not be used for coverings that you will want to launder.

MAKING WELT

If the welt will be used on an article that you plan to wash, both the cord and the fabric should be preshrunk. Simply wash and dry them as you will the finished piece.

Fabric strips for corded welt should be cut on the

bias grain so the welt is flexible and will conform to curves and corners without puckering. The stable and often somewhat stiff fabrics used for upholstery may have almost no give along the straight grainlines. For curved areas and pieces with many corners, it is essential to cut such fabrics on the bias. Yes, this takes more fabric than would be needed for cutting on the lengthwise or crosswise grain, but usually the ease of handling and finished appearance more than make up for the added fabric cost.

If the chosen fabric does stretch to some extent along the grain, and if the welt will be used mainly along straight lines, then the fabric strips might be cut on the straight grain—preferably across the fabric. In the interest of fabric economy, professional upholsterers often will cut welt strips for a project both on the bias and straight grain of the fabric, using the former for curved areas and the latter on straight lines. This works only if the pattern of the fabric looks almost the same regardless of the cut.

Cutting the Fabric

A rotary cutter and mat, used with a see-through ruler, make short work of cutting the yards and yards of welt often needed for a chair slipcover or to reupholster a couch. These tools are not expensive. They can save considerable time and produce neat, accurate results.

To determine the strip width needed, measure the circumference of the welt or piping cord and add twice the desired seam allowance. For bias-cut strips, add approximately ¼ inch (.5 cm) extra to account for the seam allowance width that will be lost due to the fabric's stretching. Chalk a line along the true bias of the fabric if strips will be cut that direction, and make the first cut. For subsequent cuts, use the edge of the ruler to guide the cutting wheel.

Sewing the Welt

Join ends of bias strips by stitching together along the fabric grain as shown in the illustration to make up the necessary length.

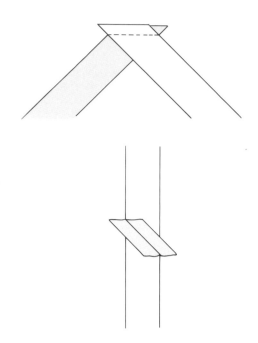

To make up the welt, fold the fabric strip right side out around a length of cord so that the long raw edges are together. Use a piping or cording presser foot, or a zipper foot, and stitch close to the cord without catching it in the seam.

Applying the Welt

When welt is incorporated into a seam that joins two pieces of fabric, first sew it to the right side of one of the pieces, again using the piping or zipper foot. Align the welt seamline along the fabric seamline with all raw edges together and sew along the welt stitching line or a thread width inside it.

When the welt is sewn, or affixed with staples, around an inner curve or corner, clip to the welt stitching line so the welt will conform to the curve without puckering. Make the clips as close together as necessary.

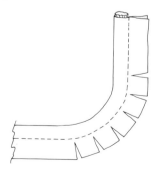

For outer corners and curves, clip V-shaped notches from the welt seam allowance to eliminate bulk.

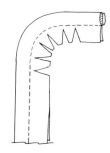

Beginnings and Endings

Where ends of the welt meet or cross a seam in the fabric piece, there are two ways to accomplish a neat finish. One method is to bend the welt across the seamline and into the seam allowance as shown. Clip a notch from the welt seam allowance just ahead of this point. After stitching, open the welt seam just to the crossed seamline and clip out the cord to reduce bulkiness. This technique is best used when the point at which the welt ends meet is out of sight or at the back of the piece.

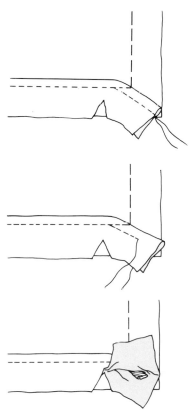

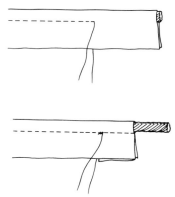

As an alternative, when the welt is continuous or the join is in a visible spot, abut the ends of the welt. Allow an extra ½ inch (1.5 cm) of welt at each end. Unstitch approximately 1 inch (3 cm) at each end of the welt seam. Fold the ends ½ inch (1.5 cm) to the inside, then stitch again along the previous stitching line. Clip away the excess cord. Attach the welt to the fabric and whipstitch the ends of the welt covering together.

Plan the placement of joins to correspond with a seamline in the fabric, if possible, or at some other point where they will not be noticed.

A welt seam is placed inconspicuously over the seamline of two front panels.

2 ▪ Tools and Equipment

Every project is more fun and goes more smoothly when you have an adequate space in which to work and have all the necessary tools within easy reach.

In addition to good lighting, sharp scissors, a working steam iron, and the basic supplies found in a reasonably well-equipped sewing room, there are other tools and accessories that are helpful or essential for making slipcovers and reupholstering furniture. Following are suggestions for some of these items, and for their use.

THE WORK AREA

Most slipcovers are large! A good-sized table is a must for laying out, cutting, arranging the pieces, pinning, and for sewing. If your sewing room or dining room can't offer this essential, consider renting a long folding table for the duration of your project.

For upholstery work you will need a table or other means of elevating the piece of furniture to a good working height. The pros use trestles—flat-topped, sawhorse-like devices that are covered with carpet fabric to prevent the piece from slipping.

SEWING MACHINE

Any sewing machine, whether a basic vintage model or state-of-the-art wonder, works best when it is free of lint build-up, properly oiled, and fitted with a new needle. These seemingly simple requirements are the most often overlooked, and cause the vast majority of stitching problems. Take a few minutes at the beginning of a project to tend to the needs of the machine and you will be rewarded.

Most slipcover fabrics and some upholstery fabrics can be sewn with a standard sewing machine that is equipped with the correct needle for the job. Some fabrics, however, demand a fairly heavy-duty machine, and the heavier upholstery fabrics require an industrial machine. If you're not certain of your machine's capabilities, buy a yard of your chosen fabric and try sewing through multiple layers to be sure the machine has the necessary power to handle the fabric.

Most sewing machines are set up for working with standard-weight sewing threads. To use heavy upholstery thread, the needle and bobbin tension will have to be adjusted. If one is available for your machine, a bobbin case made for and adjusted for heavy threads is a good investment.

One way to ensure good stitching with large, unwieldy items is to make sure both ends of the piece are supported when you sew it. That way, the machine does not have to pull pounds of cloth through the feed mechanism. It helps to place the sewing machine on a larger table than you would normally use.

Needles

Within just the last few years the selection of sewing machine needles has increased tenfold. There is a needle for every type of fabric and every thread on the market. For heavy slipcover and upholstery fabrics, there are several specialized needles that can improve the machine's performance.

Be sure that the needle you use is the *type* required by your machine. The owner's manual will specify the needle type; using the wrong one will not simply produce bad stitching, it can cause expensive damage to the machine.

Needle sizes. Not to be confused with the needle type, the size indicates the diameter of the needle and relative size of the eye. A larger needle is stronger and more capable of fast sewing through heavy fabric. For slipcover and upholstery fabrics, use the largest needle that does not leave unsightly holes in the fabric.

Sharp needles. A "standard" machine needle does not have a sharp point, but one that is slightly rounded and intended to work with average fabrics, or with most fabrics. With tightly woven cloth this universal point can be deflected by the fabric threads rather than penetrating them, producing puckered seams or skipped stitches. Sharp needles are often labeled "jeans" needles.

Coated needles. Sharp needles, particularly, often are coated to enable them to slip more smoothly through "sticky" fabrics like synthetic suede, or heavily finished fabrics, as many decorator fabrics are.

Presser Feet

Several specialty presser feet are particularly helpful with slipcover and upholstery projects.

Straight stitch foot. This foot guides the needle toward a small center hole and can prevent needle breakage. For still better results, use it with a corresponding straight stitch plate.

Piping or cording foot. With the amount of welt, or piping, a slipcover requires, investing in this foot is well worth the results. It is more effective than a zipper foot for stitching close to the cord when sewing and applying welt.

Teflon-coated foot. It is made to glide smoothly over sticky or coated fabrics, the same materials that call for a coated needle.

Blind hemmer. These are standard accessories with most machines. It takes a little practice to obtain good results with them; after that they can save hours of time.

Walking, or *even-feed foot*. This foot feeds the upper fabric layer as the feed dogs move the under layer. It is a great time-saver for matching plaids and stripes, and it works well with velvet and other fabrics that tend to scoot. A word of caution: this foot does not grip the fabric as tightly as other presser feet do, so it is especially important to make sure the fabric is supported during sewing.

THE SERGER

A slipcover project may provide the reason for buying one if you have not done so. It sews much faster than a sewing machine, and trims and overcasts seams at the same time.

As with a sewing machine, a serger performs most efficiently when it is clean, properly oiled, and supplied with new needles. Because it produces prodigious quantities of lint, a serger may require cleaning several times during a big project.

At the start of a project, check that the knife blade is sharp and free of nicks, and that the needles are in good condition. Be sure the tension is in balance; a minor maladjustment can become a major problem on a long slipcover seam.

TOOLS AND NOTIONS

In addition to the gadgets and tools available in a well-equipped sewing room, the following are especially helpful for making slipcovers and doing upholstery work.

Shears, with 10-inch (25.5-cm) blades, produce a good straight cut through heavy fabric with minimal effort.

Pinking shears are sometimes a quick alternative to machine overcasting for producing a ravel-resistant finish on slipcover seam allowances. They should not be used with synthetic fabrics.

Rotary cutter and *mat*. For fast, accurate cutting of long straight edges, particularly of the bias strips needed for welting, this is the way to go. Use a see-through ruler to guide the cutter and eliminate measuring and marking the strips as well.

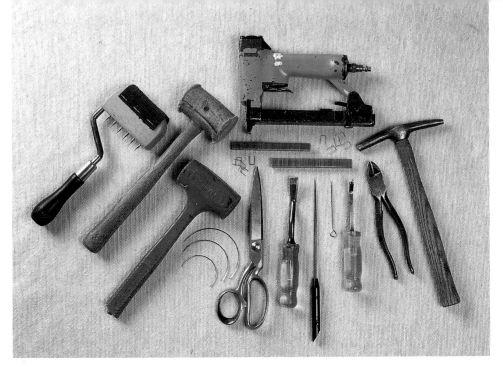

Bottom row, left to right: webbing stretcher, rawhide mallet, rubber mallet, curved hand sewing needles, shears, ripping chisel, stuffing regulator, upholstery pin, staple remover, cutting pliers, tack hammer. Above: pneumatic stapler, staples.

Hand sewing needles. For upholstery especially, buy a supply of both straight and curved heavy-duty needles in assorted sizes.

Pins for upholstery and slipcover work should have large, highly visible heads. Round-headed pins, quilters' pins, and T-pins are handy. The larger upholsterers' pins are necessary for holding heavy fabric panels in place in the course of a project.

Chalk markers, the kind that do not contain soap, are always useful. Test to be sure the marks will brush off your fabric.

Water-soluble markers work well in situations where chalk marks might be rubbed away prematurely. Always test these markers with each abric you use. Their reactions with different dyes and finishes are unpredictable.

Liquid fray retardant is a lifesaver for dealing with unintentional cuts and over-trimmed seams. It can leave a visible mark; test it with the fabric.

UPHOLSTERY TOOLS

Upholstery work calls for several tools and gadgets not usually found in a sewing room. Those listed below are highly recommended, if not essential.

Stapler. For upholstery work the heavy-duty variety is essential, an air-powered model very nice. Tool rental companies often have these at reasonable rates.

Staples $9/16$ inch (1.4 cm) and $3/8$ inch (1 cm) long are the sizes most often used for upholstery. The longer ones

are needed where the staple must penetrate several fabric layers and hold in the frame wood; the shorter for areas where the longer points might protrude to the outside of the work. Buy plenty of both.

Staple remover. Not the office variety, this sturdy one has a handle and simplifies the job of prying hundreds of staples from an upholstered piece of furniture.

Ripping chisel. This general-purpose tool is indispensable for loosening coverings, and tacked strips and fabrics.

Tack hammer. One side of the head is magnetized for use with upholstery tacks. The hammer holds the tack while it is tapped into position, eliminating bruised fingers.

Stuffing regulator. This tool resembles a slender ice pick. It is used to rearrange upholstery padding through the cover fabric.

Pliers are an aid in gripping fabric edges to pull them taut for stapling, for removing broken staples, and for pulling a needle through heavy fabric layers.

Cutting pliers are necessary when metal tack strip is used.

Mallets. Hard rubber and rawhide mallets are used to tap padded areas to even up the padding, and to hammer tacked strips and panels into place. The somewhat resilient heads don't mark the fabrics.

Webbing stretcher. The one purpose of this specialized tool is to hold webbing strips taut for stapling.

3 ▪ Cushions and Pillows

*S*eat cushions and back pillows are an integral part of many slipcover and upholstery projects. When made well they are a great complement to the couch or chair they adorn and can mean the difference between a comfortable, often-used piece of furniture and one that's strictly a showpiece. There are just a few simple tricks to creating professional-looking results.

Whether essential chair and couch cushions or frivolous accent pillows, a quick change of their covers can have an instant impact on the room's atmosphere. It's an easy and economical way to redecorate in a hurry.

THE INSIDE STORY

Most pillows or seat cushions look their best when they are plump and firmly stuffed. What goes inside is determined by the pillow's function. A seat cushion needs a firm filling that can support the weight of a body without collapsing or bottoming out. A back cushion can be a little softer.

A pillow that is stuffed with loose filling such as fiberfill or down should have a liner, an inner pillow that contains the filling. A liner can be made quickly of muslin or any scrap fabric that's handy. For a down or kapok filling, though, use a tightly woven "downproof" fabric.

Cut the covering the same size as the outer pillow cover. Sew the pieces with right sides together, leaving an opening. Turn right side out, add the filling, and stitch across the opening.

Foam

Polyurethane foam is a great choice for seat cushions. Look for a good grade of dense foam that is made especially for this purpose. The readily available inexpensive foams, such as those used for

pillow forms and bolsters, are not meant for use as seat cushions. The lighter material of which these are made will not support much weight, and will quickly lose its shape.

Polyester fiber

This material is available in batting form in several thicknesses, and as loose fiber. The batting makes a good springy surface covering for foam pillows and under upholstery. Loose fiberfill is a good, inexpensive filling for back and side cushions. And it takes a surprisingly large amount of it to stuff a pillow to the appealingly plump state.

Down and feathers

For a truly luxurious cushion, this is the filling of choice. It is a good idea to buy pre-filled pillows with downproof coverings; starting with the raw material is incredibly messy. Down and feather pillows need to be quite firm to look their best, and they require frequent plumping. On a seat cushion this filling is better used as a final layer over a foam inner cushion.

Kapok

Before polyester, kapok was a popular filling for soft cushions especially. It is also known as "vegetable down" and has some of the same characteristics as duck or goose down. It, too, is best purchased in downproof casing.

KNIFE-EDGE PILLOW

This pillow features flattened outer edges and thickness at the center. It is quick and easy to construct, and can be made with a purchased form or with any filling material. Welt or decorative cording can be incorporated into the edge seam.

1. For a purchased rectangular pillow form, measure two adjacent sides to determine the finished dimensions. So that the finished pillow looks good and plump, no ease is added. Add 1 inch (3 cm) to length and width measurements for seam allowances. Cut a paper or muslin pattern to these measurements.

2. Adjust the corners for a closer fit, if desired. Fold the pattern in half, then in half again, so that edges and corners are even. Mark a point about 3 inches (7.5 cm) from the corner on each side. Mark a point ½ inch (1.5 cm) in from the corner and equidistant from the sides. Round off the corner slightly then taper to each marked point as shown. Re-cut the pattern.

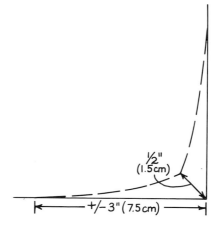

3. Use this pattern to cut the pillow front, or top.

4. For the back or underside, draw a line across the pattern to mark placement of the zipper, either at the center or near one edge. Cut the pattern apart. Cut from fabric, adding seam allowance at each cut edge.

CONSTRUCTION

1. Assemble the back. Use a zipper that is approximately 2 inches (5 cm) shorter than the length of the seam in which it will be placed. Stitch the back sections with right sides together, sewing 1 inch (2.5 cm) at each end of the seam and basting the remainder of the seam. Press open.

2. Install the zipper. Open the zipper and place it face down on the wrong side of the seam, teeth

along the seamline. Stitch along the woven line of the zipper tape from the upper end of the zipper to the lower stop. Close the zipper, stitch across the lower ends of the tape and along the remaining side. Remove the basting.

3. Stitch welt, or piping, to the wrong side of the cover front if desired, following the instructions on page 18.

4. Open the zipper and stitch the cover front to the back with right sides together.

BOX PILLOW

A box cushion or pillow is the style most often used for firm seat cushions. It can be rectangular, T-shaped, or cut to fit any chair seat. It has an inset edge strip, or boxing strip, around the perimeter. A zipper is usually installed in the boxing strip at the back of the cushion. Welt often is sewn into the edge seams to give the pillow a well-finished look.

MEASURING AND CUTTING

1. To cover a rectangular pillow, measure two adjacent sides and add 1 inch (3 cm) to each measurement for seam allowances. The total of all four side measurements is also the finished length of the boxing strip.

   For a T-shaped or irregularly shaped cushion, place the form on a sheet of paper and draw around it, then add ½ inch (1.5 cm) seam allowance all around. Carefully measure the inner line to determine the finished length of the boxing strip. For welting around the upper and lower edges, double this measurement and add seam allowances.

2. Cut the cover top and bottom from these measurements.

3. For the width of the boxing strip, measure the thickness of the cushion and add seam allowances at both long edges and at the ends.

4. Determine the length of the zipper opening. On a rectangular chair cushion the opening usually reaches all the way across the back and extends a short distance around both back corners. For a soft cushion, the opening

might be just the length of the back. It should be just long enough that the cushion can be inserted easily.

5. Divide the finished boxing strip length into two sections. For the back, use the zipper length plus 1 inch (3 cm). Then divide the width measurement in half and add ½ inch (1.5 cm) seam allowance to all edges. Cut two pieces this size.

6. For the remaining section add 2½ inches (7 cm) to the length measurement and 1 inch (3 cm) to the width. Cut one.

CONSTRUCTION

1. Place the narrow back pieces with right sides together and stitch a ½-inch (1.5-cm) seam along one long edge. Use a regular stitch length for ½ inch (1.5 cm) at each end and baste the remainder of the seam. Press open.

2. Install the zipper. Open the zipper and place it face down on the wrong side of the seam, teeth

at the seamline. Stitch along the woven line of the zipper tape from the upper end of the zipper to the lower stop. Close the zipper, stitch across the lower ends of the tape and along the remaining side. Remove the basting.

3. Stitch the zipper section to the remaining strip section at both ends with right sides together and ½-inch (1.5-cm) seams.

4. On the longer section of the strip, fold a crease across the width on the right side, ¾ inch (2 cm) from the seam, to form a pleat over the zipper end. Sew it, stitching over the previous stitching line as illustrated. Repeat for the other end of the zipper.

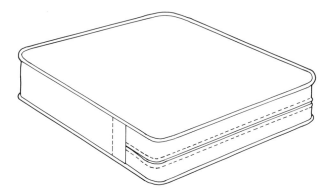

5. If welting will be added, sew it to the right side of each cover section. Detailed instructions are on page 18.

6. Working from the original finished measurements, mark a point on each edge of the boxing strip to correspond to each pillow corner.

7. On the cover sections, staystitch about 2 inches (5 cm) along the seamline on both sides of each corner. Clip the corner to the stitching.

8. With right sides together, stitch the strip to one cover section, matching marked points to corners. Stitch to the other cover section in the same way.

SOFT BOX PILLOW

This style is often used for the back cushion on chairs and couches. It is made like a knife-edge pillow, but with pleats added at the corners to define the shape. It should be stuffed with loose filling. The cover can be made removable by the addition of a zipper in the bottom seam. Use a zipper approximately 4 inches (10 cm) shorter than the seam in which it will be sewn. With a removable cover, make an inner pillow exactly the same size to contain the filling. Welt can be incorporated into the seam if this is the style of the furniture on which it will be used.

Measuring and Cutting

1. Determine the desired dimensions of the finished cushion. Because there is not a separate edge strip, the length and width measurements also include the thickness, and thickness should be added to the finished dimensions to determine the size to cut the cover. For example, for a finished pillow 20 inches (51 cm) square and 4 inches (10 cm) thick, the cover front and back should be cut 24 inches (61 cm) square plus seam allowances.

2. Cut the cover front and back to size, adding seam allowances. If an inner pillow will be used, cut pieces the same size.

3. If welt will be added, cut bias strips and make the welt according to the instructions on page 17. Total welt length should equal twice the finished length and width measurements, minus the length of the zipper.

Construction

1. Form the pleats on one cover section. Fold the piece diagonally at one corner, wrong side out, aligning the raw edges. On the raw edge, measure from the point the thickness of the pillow plus the seam allowance. Mark this point.

2. Fold the doubled fabric at the marked point, keeping the raw edges aligned.

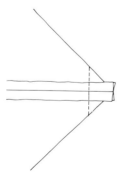

3. Pin the doubled fabric triangle to the layer of fabric under it.

4. Baste through the three fabric thicknesses.

5. Form the other three corners in the same way, alternating direction of the pleats so that the folds of the pleats at the cushion top and bottom will be toward the sides of the chair.

6. Form the pleats on the other cover section. Be sure to fold each one in the same direction as the corresponding pleat on the first cover section.

7. Install the zipper. Place one cover section inside the other, right sides together and raw edges aligned. Baste the section of seam in which the zipper will be sewn. Press the basted seam open.

8. Open the zipper and place it face down on the wrong side of the seam, teeth along the seamline. Stitch along the woven line of the zipper tape from the upper end of the zipper to the lower stop. Close the zipper, stitch across the lower ends of the tape and along the remaining side. Remove the basting.

9. Pin and stitch the remaining seams, incorporating the welt. If a zipper is not used, leave an opening on one side for turning and stuffing.

10. Make the inner pillow. Save time by omitting the corner pleats. Instead, stitch the cover sections together, leaving an opening on one edge. Fold a corner diagonally, matching the seamlines. Use a ruler to draw a line across the point at the place where the line length equals the cushion thickness. Stitch along the line as shown. Turn right side out.

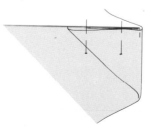

11. Fill the pillow and close the opening.

CUSHIONED CAMP STOOL

A *folding camp stool does double duty as an auxiliary*
table or extra chair when it's topped with a custom-made
box cushion.

Bold stripes around the cushion's perimeter complement
the natural linen fabric of the cover and the very short skirt.
Linen welting in a slightly darker shade matches the big
covered buttons at the pillow's center.

MATERIALS

Rectangular foam pillow form

Fabric for cover top, bottom, sides, welt,
and skirt, according to measurements

2 large buttons to cover

Straight upholstery needle or long darning
needle

MEASURING AND CUTTING

This cover was made without a zipper, but one
might be installed in the underside of the cushion,
toward one end or the other.

1. Measure and cut the cover fabrics as directed
on page 27. Cut self welt as described on
page 17.

2. To cut the skirt, determine the desired finished
length of the skirt. Double this figure and
add 1 inch (3 cm) for ½-inch (1.5-cm) seam
allowances. This will be the cutting length. For
the width of each section, add 1 inch (3 cm) to
the length measurement of one side of the
cushion. Cut two pieces this size, or four if the
pillow is square. For a rectangular cushion,
repeat for the adjacent side.

CONSTRUCTION

1. Fold under ½ inch (1.5 cm) at each end
of each skirt piece; press.

2. Fold each piece in half lengthwise, right side
out, and press along the fold.

3. Pin the strips to the right side of the cushion
bottom section before welt is attached, with
raw edges aligned and strip ends even with
corner seamline intersections. Machine baste.

4. Complete the cover according to the instructions on page 27. If there is no zipper, leave a
long opening on one edge to insert the pillow.
Trim corners and turn right side out. Put the
pillow form in place and stitch the opening
closed.

5. Cover two buttons with fabric scraps according
to package instructions.

6. With strong thread or cord, stitch the two
buttons to the cover top and bottom, stitching
them together through the cushion.

4 · Simple Cover-Ups

A new slipcover can work many kinds of magic. It will of course hide faded, outdated, or cat-damaged upholstery. It can soften the lines of a stiff and uninviting chair. It might impart a more casual look to a rather formal piece of furniture. It can give the illusion of a completely new shape to a chair with awkward lines.

In its simplest form, a slipcover might be just an especially pretty piece of fabric arranged over a footstool and tied to fit at the corners. Only a bit more complicated is a bright cover to slip over an uninteresting dining chair. Most of the designs shown in this chapter are easy to make and go together quickly. We hope they will inspire you to add your own unique variations.

The instructions are written with the thought in mind that your own candidate for re-covering probably does not look exactly like the chair or table or ottoman in the photograph. If you follow the same procedure for measuring and the same sequence for construction, you shouldn't find it a bit difficult to adapt the designs to your furnishings.

COVERS FOR STOOLS: SIMPLE AND SPECTACULAR

The quickest possible cover is an heirloom linen, smoothed over a footstool to provide a custom table just in time for tea.

Footstools, kitchen stools, low stools or high stools all respond well to quick coverings. An antique embroidered bridge cloth or the yard of fabric left over from a decorating project makes a new cover in minutes.

Knot the corners, tie them with lengths of decorative cord, or keep them in place with big colorful buttons. Sew a bright ribbon along the center of each side, with long ends to tie in corner fullness.

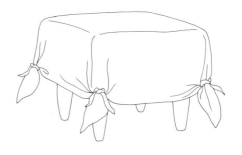

PILLOW-TOPPED STOOL

*T*his clever design is easy to assemble. The soft pillow tied on top provides a comfortable place to rest weary feet or for a cat to nap.

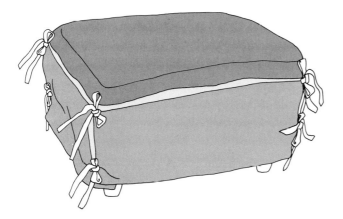

MATERIALS

Three complementary fabrics are used: one for the pillow; a second for the cover, top and skirt, and the ties; the third for the overskirt. Measure the stool according to the instructions to determine the amount of each fabric that will be needed. You'll also need soft fiberfill or other stuffing for the pillow.

INSTRUCTIONS

1. Measure the width and length of the stool top. Determine the desired finished length for the skirts.

2. Add seam allowance at all sides and cut two pieces this size for the pillow and one for the cover top.

3. For the skirt, add seam allowance and 1½ inches (4 cm) hem allowance to the finished skirt length measurement. Cut two pieces this length and the same width the cover top was cut. Cut two the same length, and the width of the cover top cut length measurement.

4. Cut the overskirt pieces the same length as the skirt. In width, add 2 inches (5 cm) to the width and length measurements from step 1 and cut two pieces each size.

5. Cut 16 strips for ties, 2½ inches (6 cm) wide and 18 inches (46 cm) long.

6. Make the ties. For eight of the strips, press each end of each strip ½ inch (1 cm) to the wrong side; press. For the other eight strips, finish only one end. Fold in half lengthwise, right side out. Press. Fold the raw edges into the center crease and press. Stitch both long edges of each strip, and stitch the finished ends.

7. Make the pillow. Pin an unfinished tie end at each corner on the right side of one pillow section, raw edge of the tie at the pillow corner. Baste, stitching diagonally across the corners. Sew the cover sections with right sides together, keeping the tie ends free, and following the basting stitching at the corners. Leave an opening on one side. Trim the corners and turn right side out. Fill the pillow, and close the opening.

8. Stitch an unfinished tie end to the right side of the cover top, as for the pillow.

9. With right sides together, stitch the skirt sections together at the ends.

10. Press and stitch a ¾-inch (2-cm) double hem around the lower edge.

11. Press and stitch a ¾-inch (2 cm) double hem at the lower edge and at each side of each overskirt section.

12. Mark the placement point for the corner ties on the overskirt sides, measuring up from the hemmed edges. At each marked point, stitch a tie to the hem on the wrong side, stitching an X pattern.

13. With right sides together, center an overskirt section on each side of the cover top (skirt sections won't be as wide as the sides of the top). Baste.

14. Pin the skirt to the cover top and overskirt, right side of the skirt to the wrong side of the overskirt sections. Match the seams to the corners. On the corners of the top, clip almost to the seamline as necessary to fit the skirt. Stitch, keeping the tie ends free.

15. Tie the pillow to the cover top, then place the cover over the stool and tie the overskirt at the corners.

FITTED COVER

A simple-to-sew cover takes on quite a personality when it features a variety of patterns or colors.

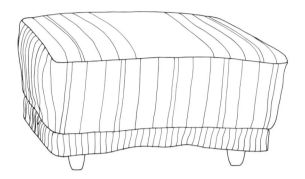

INSTRUCTIONS

1. Measure the length and width of the stool. Add seam allowance at each side and cut a rectangle for the top.

2. Place the piece on the stool and round the corners slightly to fit.

3. Determine the length of the skirt; add seam allowance top and bottom.

4. For the skirt width, measure the circumference of the stool near the top. Add seam allowance at both sides.

5. Cut the skirt to these measurements.

6. With right sides together, stitch the sides together, forming a tube. Plan to locate the seam at one corner and use the top measurements to mark the other corners.

7. For the edging length, double the planned finished length and add twice the seam allowance.

8. Cut the strip this length and to the width determined in step 4.

9. Stitch the ends as for the skirt.

10. Fold the edging in half, right side out, aligning the raw edges. Press.

11. Stitch to the lower edge of the skirt with right sides together.

12. Sew the skirt to the top with right sides together, matching the corner markings to the corners.

DINING CHAIR COVERS IN MELON COLORS

Color variety makes a refreshing change from all-of-a-kind chairs in the dining room. These covers are easy to fit and to sew; each has just three pieces.

Since you are making several covers of the same size and shape, it is quicker to cut a sample cover from inexpensive muslin and use it as a pattern. Cut the pieces out roughly, leaving generous margins. Pin the cover together on the chair and machine baste it together to check the fit.

Measuring and Cutting

Measure the chair according to the instructions on page 48, with these adjustments:

1. Measure the seat to include the skirt length at both sides and at the front. The seat extends to the back of the back legs and rails, with slight ease added at the depth of each side.

2. The inner back includes the depth of the sides and slight ease to match that of the seat. At the top, include the depth of the upper back in the inner back measurement.

3. On the outer back, add extra length so the lower edge can be matched to the seat/skirt pieces when the cover is pinned.

Cut the three pieces, oversized, from muslin.

Construction

1. Fit the inner back to the chair. Pin darts at the upper front corners, leaving ample seam allowance around the back of the piece.

2. Fit the outer back. Pin around the edges to the inner back.

3. Fit the seat/skirt section. Pin to the inner and outer back. Pin darts at front corners.

4. Machine baste. Stitch the four darts first, then the seams.

5. Try the cover for fit and mark the hem. Mark matching points and seamlines on the muslin. Trim seam and hem allowances.

6. Take apart the muslin and press the pieces to use as patterns.

Options

It would be a simple matter to add a long skirt for a more formal look. Use the outer back measurement and the circumference of the short skirt at the lower edge to determine the width of the skirt extension. For a gathered skirt, allow approximately one and one-half times the width measurement. For a more tailored look, add a box pleat at each front corner. Plan for a pleat depth of 3 to 4 inches (8 or 10 cm). For pleat variations, see page 40.

Sunshine-Striped Chair Cover

*A*wning stripes in cheerful colors perk up a simple wooden chair.

This simple cover fits a straight chair with a round seat. A box pleat at the center of the back provides ease of fit. Matching ties keep the pleat neatly closed and add an element of interest. A striped pattern like this looks its best if the stripes are matched across the upper back seam.

MEASURING AND CUTTING

Measure the chair and cut the fabric according to the instructions on page 48, with the following changes.

1. For a round seat, make a paper pattern. Place a sheet of newspaper on the seat and mark the outline of the seat with a thumbnail. Fold the paper in half, side to side, and even up the edges before cutting. On each side of the pattern mark the outer edges of the back at the points where the back joins the seat. Measure around the front of the seat between the two marked points to determine the width of the skirt. Add seam allowance around the edge to cut fabric.

2. Determine the skirt length. Add hem allowance at the lower edge and seam allowance at the upper edge. Add twice the seam allowance to the width measurement.

3. Inner back width at the seat will be the measurement, at the seamline, between the marks on the seat pattern. The upper back may be different. Add seam allowance at all edges.

4. The outer back length equals the inner back length plus the skirt length. In width, allow for a center back box pleat using one of the methods described on page 40. A pleat depth of 4 inches (10 cm) at each side would be a good average for this chair.

5. For ties, cut two pieces 19 inches (49 cm) long and 2¼ inches (7 cm) wide. This includes ½ inch (1.5 cm) seam allowance at each end and ¼ inch (.5 cm) on the long edges.

CONSTRUCTION

1. Make the ties. Fold each strip in half lengthwise, right sides together, and stitch the long edge and across one end. Turn and press. Fold under the seam allowance on the other end and press.

2. Form or stitch the box pleat at center back according to the instructions for the variation you chose, adding the ties.

3. With right sides together, sew the inner back to the seat between the marked points.

4. Stitch the skirt to the seat.

5. Stitch the inner back to the outer back.

6. Press and stitch the hem.

TAILORED STRIPES

Striped fabric is a perfect choice for this well-mannered cover. At the backs, contrasting ribbon threads through grommets along the pleat to provide a tailored finish.

In addition to the fabric for each cover, you will need large grommets and a grommet attachment tool, and a length of color-coordinated ribbon or cord.

MEASURING AND CUTTING

With several chairs alike, it is easiest to make the first cover of inexpensive muslin, check the fit, then take it apart and use it as a pattern. Measure the chair and cut the cover pieces according to the instructions on page 48 with the following changes.

1. Include the depth (thickness) of the chair back in the inner back width measurement. Add the upper back depth to the top of the inner back piece.

2. On the outer back, plan to add the Quick Box Pleat according to the instructions on page 40. Adjust the pleat depth to accommodate the stripe pattern and to allow matching the inner and outer back sections at the upper seam.

3. For the seat/front piece, add measurements D and E.

4. For the width of the side skirt sections, use the seat depth plus the depth of the inner back at the seat.

Add seam and hem allowances before cutting from fabric.

CONSTRUCTION

1. Form the pleat in the outer back section. Don't stitch it along the center back, but do topstitch along the center back creases. Baste the pleat across the upper edge and trim the upper back.

2. Stitch the darts at the upper corners of the inner back.

3. Stitch the inner back to the seat across the back, stitching just to the seat seamlines.

4. With the pieces on the chair, pin the side skirt sections to the front, rounding the corners to fit. Stitch, continuing the stitching along the seat/skirt seam to the seat back.

5. Stitch this piece to the inner back.

6. Press and stitch the hem.

7. Mark positions for the grommets, placing them approximately ¼ inch (.7 cm) from the fold of the pleat. Attach the grommets and thread the ribbon through them.

Pleat Variations

A box pleat can provide ease down the back of a chair cover or at corners of the seat or skirt. Two of the methods below include separate underlays, which allow you to add a different pattern or color to personalize the cover design in your own way.

Regardless of the variation you choose, cut the pieces with extra allowance at the upper edge. Stitch and fold the pleat, baste across the upper edge seamline, then cut the edge to size through all thicknesses. The instructions involve stitching the upper few inches of the pleat closed. Change or omit this step if it doesn't suit your design or your chair.

QUICK BOX PLEAT

The simplest box pleat is made by extending the fabric at center back, at a corner, or wherever the pleat will be. At the appropriate place, add four times the pleat depth to the width of the piece. For example, to add a box pleat at the center back of a chair cover, for a pleat depth of 4 inches (10 cm) on each side add a total of 16 inches (40 cm) at the center back. If the piece is cut with the pattern center back line on folded fabric, add 8 inches (20 cm) at center back for the pleat.

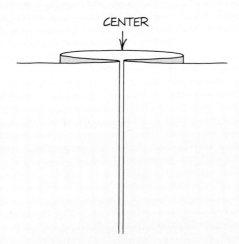

CENTER

1. Cut the back as described above. Mark the center back and pleat foldlines on each side at the upper and lower edges.

2. Fold the piece right side out to bring the center back marks together.

3. Stitch down 4 to 6 inches (10 to 15 cm) from the upper edge along the center back line to close the upper part of the pleat, if desired.

4. Fold the pleat to even depth at both sides of center back; press. Baste across the upper edge.

5. For pronounced creases along the outer folds of the pleat, edgestitch along the creases.

6. To add ties, finish both ends of the tie sections and stitch opposite one another to the underside of the center creases as shown.

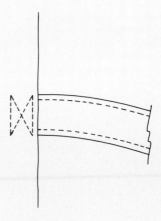

PLEAT WITH SEPARATE UNDERLAY AND CENTER BACK SEAMS

A box pleat in which a separate piece of fabric is used for the underlay and inner pleat allows for sewing ties or other fasteners into the seam at center back.

1. Plan a seam at center back of the outer back cover piece.

2. Determine the pleat depth. Cut the underlay four times this width plus twice the seam allowance, and the same length as the outer back. Match the upper back line to that of the cover back. Mark the center back.

3. Pin ties at the desired points along the center back seamline of each back section, raw ends aligned with center back edges.

4. Stitch the underlay to the back sections at center back along both seamlines, with right sides together. Press the seams toward the underlay.

5. On the inside, bring the seamlines together and stitch down approximately 4 inches (10 cm) from the upper edge, stitching along the previous stitching line.

6. On the outside, fold the underlay to form even pleats at each side of center. Press the folds.

7. If desired, topstitch along the outer folds. Or topstitch just the inner folds for a softer outside pleat.

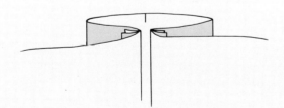

PLEAT WITH SEPARATE UNDERLAY SEAMED AT THE EDGES

The seams of this pleat are at the inner creases.

1. In width, cut the underlay twice the desired pleat depth plus twice the seam allowance.

2. On each half of the outer back section (or other piece to be pleated) extend the width at center back by the pleat depth plus seam allowance.

3. Cut the pieces and mark center back on each.

4. With right sides together stitch the underlay to each half of the back along the long edges.

5. On the right side, fold each back section at the marks to form pleats that meet at center back. Pin and stitch along the center back line to approximately 4 inches (10 cm) below the upper edge.

6. Press the creases, if desired, and edgestitch close to the folds.

7. To add ties, stitch as shown in the illustration with the Quick Pleat, opposite.

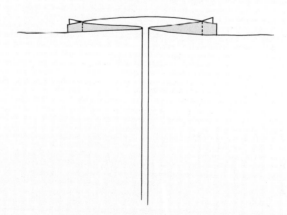

There are all sorts of ways to keep the folds of the pleat together at center back. As an alternative to the ties described above, try the buttons and buttonholes shown on pages 76 and 77.

A BEDROOM IN BLUE AND WHITE

*C*overs and pillows in a duet of blue and white patterns make a well-coordinated room from furniture odds and ends.

CHAIR COVER

A straight chair with an upholstered seat is dressed up quickly with this easy-to-make cover. The seat and skirt front are a single piece of fabric. Extensions at the skirt sides and at the lower front and back edges form pleats for added ease and style.

MEASURING AND CUTTING

Measure the chair according to the instructions on page 48, with changes.

1. Measure the inner back width to include depth, or thickness, of the sides and depth at the upper back.

2. On the outer back, place a mark at each side to indicate the top of the seat. From a point ½ inch (1.5 cm) above this mark to the lower edge, extend the width of the piece by 5 inches (12 cm) at each side to make the pleat extensions.

3. For the seat/front piece, place a mark at each side to indicate the front edge of the seat. From a point ½ inch (1.5 cm) above this mark to the lower edge, extend the width of the piece by 5 inches (12 cm) at each side.

4. For the side skirt width, measure from the front of the chair seat to the back of the chair. Add 5 inches (12 cm) at each side. Don't add seam allowance at the sides when cutting. Cut two.

5. Add seam allowances or hem allowances to all pieces for cutting, omitting seam allowance on the back and front pleat extensions.

6. For ties, cut four pieces 6 inches (15 cm) wide and 36 inches (90 cm) long. Measurements include ¼ inch (.5 cm) seam allowances.

CONSTRUCTION

1. Make the ties. For each tie, fold the fabric in half lengthwise, wrong side out. Stitch the long edges together and stitch across one end. Turn and press.

2. With the piece on the chair, pin darts at upper corners of the inner back. Stitch.

3. With right sides together, stitch the long edges of the lower front pleat extensions to skirt side pleat extensions, stitching from marked points to the lower edge. Stitch across the pleat upper edges to the marked points.

4. Stitch the outer back pleat extensions to the sides in the same way.

5. Stitch the outer and inner back sections with right sides together to the marked points on the back.

6. Stitch the inner back to the seat, keeping the pleats free and clipping to the seamline at the marked points as necessary.

7. Pin the unfinished tie ends, one on top of the other, close to the back on skirt upper edges, raw edges aligned. Stitch the skirt sides to the seat sides and inner back between the marked points.

8. Fold the pleats toward the back and toward the front. If desired, stitch them in place through the upper seam allowances.

9. Press and stitch a hem around the lower edge.

To make the striped pillow, refer to the instructions for a knife-edge pillow, page 26.

Dressing Table Cover

Start with any sort of table, add a pretty cover, top it with a protective sheet of glass, and it's the perfect place for a young girl to dream of the future.

MEASURING AND CUTTING

1. For the cover top, measure the length and width of the table top and add seam allowance at all sides.

2. For the skirt, plan a 4-inch (10-cm) box pleat at each corner. For the skirt width, use the top circumference measurement and add 64 inches plus seam allowance. To the length measurement, add seam allowance at the upper edge and hem allowance at the bottom. Cut fabric lengths to make up the total width needed, planning piecing seams to be inside the pleats if possible.

3. For ties, cut four pieces 6 inches (15 cm) wide and 36 inches (90 cm) long. Measurements include ¼ inch (.5 cm) seam allowances.

CONSTRUCTION

1. Make the ties. For each tie, fold the fabric in half lengthwise, wrong side out. Stitch the long edges and stitch across one end. Turn and press. Turn the unfinished ends ½ inch (1.5 cm) to the inside; press.

2. Stitch lengthwise skirt seams; press.

3. Form the corner pleats with the skirt around the table. Stitch each in place across the upper edge.

4. Press and stitch the hem.

5. Mark positions for the ties on the pleat folds. Pin the unfinished end of one tie under the fold of each pleat. Stitch in place, stitching an X pattern.

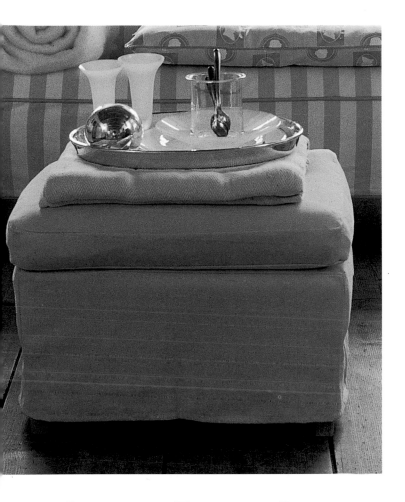

3. For the cushion side, cut a strip equal in length o twice the combined length and width of the cushion top piece. In width, cut it the cushion thickness plus double the seam allowance.

4. For the ottoman, measure the circumference around the top and add twice the seam allowance. This will be the cutting width.

5. For the length, determine the desired finished length, add hem allowance, and add 3 inches (8 cm). Cut fabric to these measurements.

CONSTRUCTION

1. Make the cushion cover. Stitch the ends of the edge strip together. With the seam at one corner, mark the other corner positions on the seamline of each long edge, using the cover top as a guide.

2. Stitch a cover underside section to each side of the edge strip, ending the stitching at each corner seamline.

3. Place this piece on the cushion, wrong side out. Pin a diagonal seam at each corner to miter the corners. Remove the cover and stitch the seams.

4. Stitch the cover top to the edge strip, matching corners.

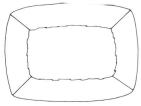

5. Make the ottoman cover. Stitch the ends with right sides together.

6. Hem the lower edge.

7. Place the cover on the ottoman, wrong side out. Pin a dart at each corner to miter the corners. The width of the border around the top should equal the width of the cushion underside pieces.

8. Remove the cover and stitch the darts.

9. With right sides together, pin the cushion cover underside to the ottoman top around the inner raw edges. Stitch.

10. Put the cushion into its cover, and the cover over the ottoman.

CUSHION-TOPPED OTTOMAN

*W*ith its clean lines and pure white linen fabric, *this ottoman cover is simplicity itself. An attached top cushion adds just enough height so that the ottoman can double as a table when the need arises.*

MEASURING AND CUTTING

Add ½ inch (1.5 cm) where seam allowances are indicated.

1. For the cushion top, measure the cushion width and length. Add seam allowance at all sides and cut the piece. Round the corners as necessary to match the cushion.

2. For the underside of the cushion, cut two pieces equal in length to the length of the cushion top piece, and 3½ inches (9 cm) wide. Cut two pieces equal in length to the width of the cushion top, and 3½ inches (9 cm) wide.

DRAPED LINEN

Natural linen fabric, generous width across the back, and extra length all contribute to the elegant appearance of this distinctive cover.

Because of the chair's curved upper back, the cover back hangs slightly on the bias—a nice effect with no extra effort. That same curve could make it tricky to achieve an even hemline, but with the extended length a little hemline variance won't be noticed. Deep pleats add fullness at the back and the tie belt keeps it in place.

MEASURING AND CUTTING

Refer to the instructions on page 48 to measure the chair and cut the pieces, making the changes indicated below. For the skirt length, add approximately 3 inches (8 cm) to the floor-length skirt measurement. Add seam and hem allowances when cutting.

1. Include the depth (thickness) of the chair back in the inner back width, and add the depth to the top of the inner back piece.

2. For the outer back, plan a pleat at each side, adding approximately 12 inches (30 cm) in width for each pleat. Cut from the top to the desired finished length, plus seam and hem allowances. Cut the upper back line roughly, adding extra seam allowance, then trim it to shape after the pleats are made.

3. Cut the seat using just the seat top measurements.

4. For the skirt front, use the seat width measurement for the upper edge width. At the lower edge, add approximately 2 inches (5 cm) in width at the hemline on each side. Taper to the upper width to determine the side seamlines.

5. For the skirt side, include the depth of the chair back in the width measurement. At the front seamline, taper outward at the hemline as for the skirt front.

6. For ties, cut two pieces 4½ inches (11.5 cm) and 40 inches (1 m) long. Measurements include ¼-inch (.5-cm) seam allowances.

CONSTRUCTION

1. Fold each tie section in half with right sides together. Stitch the long edges and across one end. Turn and press.

2. Form the pleats at the upper edge of the outer back, with creases toward the sides. Baste across the pleats and cut the upper edge to size.

3. Stitch the inner back to the seat back, stitching between the seat back seamlines.

4. Stitch the side and front skirt sections together.

5. Sew the skirt to the seat and inner back, matching skirt seams to seat front corners.

6. Pin the unfinished tie ends to the right side of the outer back at about seat level, aligning raw edges.

7. Stitch the outer back to the inner back/skirt, keeping the tie ends free.

8. Press and stitch the hem.

Making Covers
for Straight Chairs

Use the diagram as a guide for measuring a straight chair
and figuring fabric requirements for the cover. Even if your
chair does not look exactly like the one pictured, most of
the components should be the same.

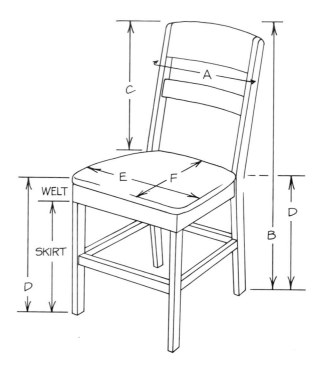

A. *Chair back*, from midpoint of side rail around the
front or back to the midpoint of the other side rail.
Make separate measurements at top and at seat
if the width is different at the top and bottom.

For some cover styles, the inner back cover section
extends to include the sides. In this case the width
of the side rails is included in the inner back
measurement.

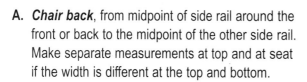

B. *Height of the chair*, from top center back to
the floor. Measure straight down even when
the chair back curves inward; that is the way
the cover will hang.

C. *Height of the back*, from top of seat. Measure
both at the sides and center if the upper back
is shaped.

D. *Top of the seat to the floor.* If the cover
will have a welt with an attached skirt,
divide the D measurement as desired.

E. *Width of the seat.* Measure at both
front and back if necessary.

F. *Depth of the seat*, from front to back.

G. *Circumference of chair at the seat base*,
including side rails and legs.

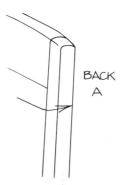

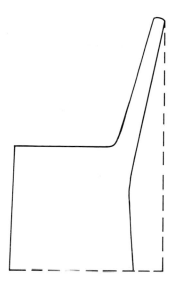

For a floor-length cover especially, the fabric will hang more gracefully if the cover is cut straight down from the top of the chair back. This means adding width at the sides, and will affect both the A and G measurements. The added fullness can be taken in with ties at the back corners, with a back belt, or in all sorts of imaginative ways. Weight a string and tape it to the top of the chair back, then measure the sides according to this "plumb line" as shown.

For a shorter skirt, add extra hem allowance. Measure up from the floor to even the hemline.

A separate side section or gusset will be indicated for some chairs or some cover designs. In this case, don't include the depth of the rails in the A measurement, but measure separately, adding ease as needed. This measurement usually will be wider at the top than at the bottom of the back.

CUTTING THE COVER

In most cases it is easiest to cut and pin the cover on the chair itself, wrong side out. This allows you to see where and how much ease should be added at different points, and to accommodate irregularities in the chair's shape. Best, it allows you to sew the cover together with little repinning.

If you are making covers for a set of chairs, or if this is your first try at slipcovers, make a test cover of inexpensive muslin and machine baste it together. Check the fit, then take the cover apart to use as a pattern.

The chapter on making tailored slipcovers, beginning on page 53, offers much information that can be equally helpful when the project is a simple unstructured cover.

Add seam allowances as you cut. A good standard is ½ inch (1.5 cm). Add more in places where you anticipate fitting difficulties, but mark the seamlines in those areas as a reminder when you stitch the cover. Add hem allowance to all pieces that extend to the lower edge of the cover.

The project, or your chair, might call for exceptions to the following generic cutting instructions.

1. *Inner back.* Use measurements A and C. Mark center at top and bottom.

2. *Outer back.* Use measurements A and B. Mark center at top and bottom. Add a pleat allowance or plan for a seam at center back if the design calls for it.

3. *Seat.* Use measurements E and F. Ease should not usually be added to this piece. Mark center front and back. Mark corners on the seamlines.

4. *Skirt.* Divide the D measurement into welt and lower skirt sections if necessary. The welt seamlines should match those of the seat. For the skirt, add width for gathers or pleat allowance at corners. Mark centers and corners on all pieces.

CAPTAIN'S CHAIR IN FULL DRESS

*D*ecked out in its bright cotton cover, the captain's chair earns an on-the-spot promotion. Corner pleats, the back ones tied in place, add just the right amount of fullness to the graceful long skirt.

This cover can be fitted with a seat cushion in place if your chair includes one. For a cushioned seat, add a tuck-in allowance of 6 inches (15 cm) to the seat sides and back, and to the lower edges of the inner back and inner arms. Some of the techniques used to make this cover are illustrated in Chapter 5, page 53.

Measure and cut the cover according to the instructions on page 48, with the changes noted below. Cut the pieces roughly, with additional seam and hem allowance, and pin-fit the cover on the chair.

MEASURING AND CUTTING

1. Include the depth of the side rails in the inner front measurement.

2. On the outer back, mark a point on each side approximately 6 inches (15 cm) below the top of the arm. Below this point, cut the piece 4 inches (10 cm) wider at each side for a pleat extension.

3. Use the seat width and depth dimensions for the seat cover section.

4. For the skirt front, add 4 inches (10 cm) at each side for pleat extensions. For length, measure from the seat front edge.

5. Cut two inner arm pieces. Measure the length from the seat over the arm to its outer edge. The width equals the seat depth.

6. Cut two outer arm sections. For length, measure from the outer edge of the arm to the desired finished length. For width, measure from the front of the seat to the back of the chair (seat depth plus back thickness). At the back corner, mark a point to correspond to the mark on the outer back and add the same

pleat extension below the mark. Add a pleat extension at the front corner too.

7. For ties, cut four pieces, each 18 inches (46 cm) in length and 2½ inches (6.5 cm) wide. Measurements include ¼-inch (.5 cm) seam allowances.

CONSTRUCTION

1. Make the ties. Fold each strip in half lengthwise, wrong side out. Stitch the long edges and across one end. Turn and press. Turn the unfinished ends to the inside; press

2. Fit the cover on the chair wrong side out. Pin darts at the front corners of the inner arm sections. Pin darts at the upper corners of the inner back section. Fit the outer and inner back sections, then the inner arms, seat, and outer arms. Add the front. Pin all seams except at the corner pleats.

3. Carefully remove the cover. Stitch the darts. Stitch the long edges of the pleat extensions together at each front corner. Stitch across the top of each pleat to the seamline marks.

4. Stitch the remaining seams, beginning with the seat seams. Incorporate the upper edges of the pleat extensions in the seam at the front corners.

5. Sew the inner back/inner arm seams next, then the outer/inner arm seams. Stitch the outer arms and inner back to the outer back above the pleat markings.

6. Press and stitch the hem.

7. Mark tie placement points several inches below the upper edge of each back pleat. Pin the unfinished end of a tie section to the underside of each pleat fold. Stitch in place with an X.

5 ▪ Making a Tailored Slipcover

Slipcovers give new life to old furniture just as reupholstering will do, but without the task of stripping off the original covering. A well-fitted cover is sometimes difficult to distinguish from upholstery, but a slipcover can be removed for laundering or dry cleaning.

Even tailored, close-fitting slipcovers are not difficult to make. It is essential, though, to have ample work space. You need a sewing machine that isn't intimidated by multiple layers of fabric, and you need a good-sized table for arranging and for sewing.

EASY OR CHALLENGING?

As with almost any project, a slipcover can be as painless or as difficult an experience as you make it. The biggest difference between the two extremes is your choice of fabric. Try—*try*—to notice more about the chosen fabric than just its perfect color or gorgeous pattern. To expedite the work, consider these factors too:

Fiber content. Medium-weight cotton and cotton blended with linen or with a small percentage of synthetic fiber are probably the easiest materials to sew. Synthetics can be slippery and difficult to manage. For detailed information, see Chapter 1.

Patterns. Solid-colored fabric, of course, is easiest. Large prints and plaids that require matching will require considerably more time than will small patterns, checks, or stripes that look good without being matched. In addition, a printed pattern that is not symmetrical or not clearly visible on the wrong side of the fabric will make it necessary to cut the slipcover right side out and then re-pin all the seams before sewing. If a stripe or plaid is your heart's desire, try to choose one that is even, that "reads" the same from left to right as from right to left.

Nap. One-way fabrics such as corduroy or velvet require a little extra care in that all pieces must be cut with the same orientation. A plain weave fabric—one that looks the same from any direction—speeds up planning and cutting and can require less yardage.

The fray factor. If you plan a washable slipcover, choose a fabric that ravels minimally. You won't have to overcast seams.

PLANNING THE COVER

Make note of the seamlines and other construction details if you are covering an upholstered piece. It is usually a good idea to plan seams in the slipcover at the same places. You can use the upholstery as a guide to design details too, such as size and placement of welting, cushion style, skirt length, and so on. Or you can improve upon those features that don't delight you. The upholstery may have a channeled back, or non-functional seams, or some other feature that you can simply omit from your plan.

Some elements will have to change. You'll need a zipper or other type of closure. For a chair, a zipper at one back corner is standard. A couch should have one at each corner.

MATERIAL REQUIREMENTS

Fabric shops specializing in decorator fabrics have pictorial charts that will give you an approximate idea of the amount of fabric you will need. It is essential, though, to measure your own furniture carefully before you buy.

Measure the length and width of each separate section of the chair or couch as shown in the diagram. Your own piece may have more or fewer sections. Record the measurements of each fabric panel, and indicate the quantity of each one that will be needed. Be sure to include tuck-in and seam allowances. Measure the total yardage of welt if it is used. If there is a skirt, measure the length and circumference, and make note of the number and depth of any pleats.

Fabric panels normally are cut with their vertical orientation on the lengthwise grain, with the pattern direction as indicated by the arrows in the diagrams. In other words, a pattern should read upward on the most visible areas: the inner and outer back, outer arms, and front. This also means that nap direction, as on velvet or corduroy, will be just the opposite—it will be smooth in the downward direction.

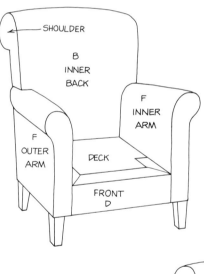

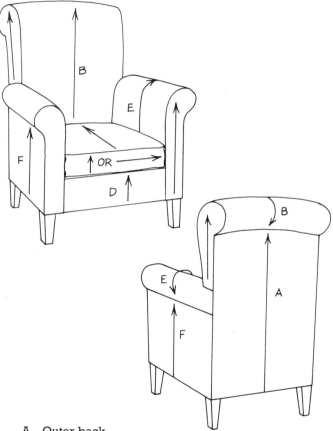

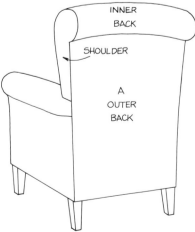

A Outer back

B Inner back. Add 6 inches (15cm) tuck-in.

C Deck (Alternate fabric can be substituted.) Add tuck-in.

D Front

E Inner arm (also the wing, if present). Add tuck-in.

F Outer arm (also the wing).

G Arm front

H Seat cushion - top and bottom, boxing strip

I Back cushion - front and back, boxing strip

J Skirt

K Welt

For a couch slipcover, you can **save** considerable yardage—and time—if the fabric can be "railroaded," or cut with the lengthwise grain running the width of the couch. This way, the outer and inner back pieces can each be cut as a single piece. The technique won't work with directional patterns or napped fabrics, or with fabric that stretches considerably along the crossgrain. Some decorator fabrics are made with railroading in mind, for example with stripes woven across the width instead of lengthwise.

To figure the needed fabric yardage, draw a diagram of the pieces and their measurements, allowing generous seam and hem allowances in your plan. Decide how the lower edge will be finished. Determine whether you can cut the welt strips from scraps or whether extra yardage will be needed.

Napped fabrics and patterns, stripes, or plaids that require matching will require additional yardage. It helps to know the size of a pattern repeat when you do your layout. Generally, add the length of the pattern repeat for each full-sized piece you will cut.

Always buy a yard or two extra. Think of it as an insurance payment. If you don't need it for the cover, it can be used for extra pillows, arm covers, a spare cushion cover, or can be saved for an emergency repair.

PREPARING THE FABRIC

To make a slipcover that can be washed, the fabric should be washed and dried to preshrink it, then carefully pressed before it is cut. This may not be a simple matter with a length of fabric intended to cover two love seats.

An alternative is to buy a yard of fabric and measure its dimensions accurately, then wash and dry it to note the shrinkage. If there is only minimal shrinkage, note the direction in which the shrinkage occurs and allow for it when you cut. Another option is to have a dry cleaner steam shrink the cloth for you.

CUTTING AND FITTING THE SLIPCOVER

The photo section that follows shows the cutting of a slipcover for a couch. The procedure for a chair is exactly the same—it's just shorter. Your chair or couch may not look like the model here, but the basic steps are the same for almost any style or shape. Look at the photos in the upholstery section on page 103 for some additional tips and techniques.

The fabric chosen for the cover is a medium-weight, plain weave cotton. It has no nap and is stable enough that it can be railroaded. It's a perfect fabric for the job. The piece was machine washed and dried to preshrink it. It was ironed to ensure that it will be straight for cutting, but most likely will not need ironing after future launderings.

The cover will be cut and fitted directly on the couch. Because the fabric is a solid color and the couch is symmetrical, the cover can be pinned

wrong side out. If welt will be used in some of the seams, those will have to be unpinned later to add the welt. The remaining seams are ready for sewing.

Except as noted, the pieces will be cut with the lengthwise grain of the fabric perpendicular to the floor.

1. Mark skirt placement.

If a skirt will be added to a chair or couch that does not have one, chalk-mark a line around the piece to indicate the skirt placement line. Measure up from the floor.

The best skirt length is a matter of preference and depends upon the style of the furniture. Experiment with different lengths to see which works best with your piece. For a chair or couch with a spring front edge, the skirt seamline cannot be above the breakaway at the front/arm join.

Our slipcover candidate is—well—rather shabby. It has a good, solid frame, though, and the springs are firm. A comparable new couch would cost many times the price of a new cover. This couch will not be seen again without a cover, so the torn upholstery was given only a quick fix with cloth tape.

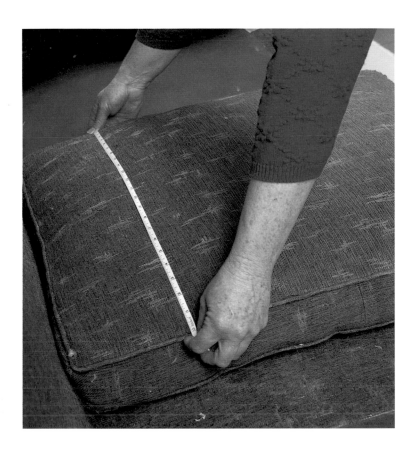

2. Measure the seat cushions.

Measure two seat cushions; the center one often is slightly different. Add seam allowance ($\frac{1}{2}$ inch or 1.5 cm is standard), and cut the cover top and bottom. For the boxing strip, measure the width and perimeter. Add seam allowance at all sides to cut the pieces. Cut the top and bottom with the lengthwise grain front to back. Generally, the boxing strip should be cut with the lengthwise grain as the height of the strip. For a stable, solid-colored fabric like that used here, it could be cut either way.

For a T-shaped or L-shaped cushion, lay the fabric on the cushion and feel your way around the edge seam with a chalk marker. Cut with extra seam allowance to allow for fit adjustments.

3. Measure the back cushions.

Measure and cut the back cushion covers the same way. Each piece of the slipcover is first blocked out; that is, cut as a rough rectangle with several inches of margin except at predictable straight edges. Use large T-pins or upholstery pins to secure fabric to the furniture for cutting.

If no skirt will be added, or if lightweight fabric is used for a cover with a skirt, add 6 to 8 inches (15 to 20 cm) in length to all pieces that extend to the lower edge of the chair or couch. The lower edge of a cover with a skirt can be finished to secure under the furniture to keep the cover in place. For a hemmed cover, the additional length provides for a doubled hem. The cover fabric for the couch in the photos is heavy enough that, with the skirt added, the extra security measure won't be necessary.

4. Cut the outer back.

To railroad the fabric, as shown, run the fabric from end to end. To run the fabric vertically, plan seams as they are located on the upholstery. Usually back seams correspond to the points at which cushions meet; sometimes there is just one seam at the center. Add 6 inches (15 cm) at each end to accommodate the zippers.

5. Position the inner back piece.

In this case, it can be cut from the same fabric length used for the outer back. Match to the outer back edge across the top. At the deck or platform edge, both seam allowance and tuck-in allowance are added.

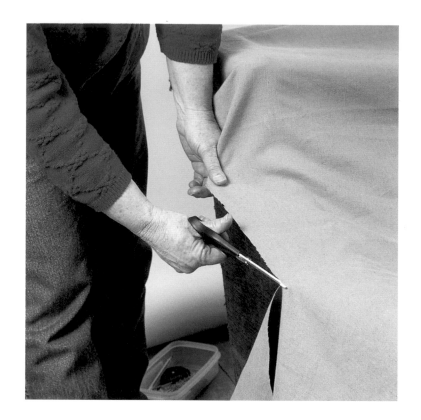

The ends of the inner back section are cut roughly at the arm edges. This will allow enough fabric for fitting around the inner arm and or tuck-in at the lower corner.

The addition of a tuck-in allowance keeps the cover from tearing when weight is placed on it and helps keep the cover neatly in place. The amount of tuck-in allowance to add depends upon the distance the couch will depress at the breakaway points where the front edge and inner arms meet.

If there is a firm front edge and firm joint at that point, taper the tuck-in from almost nothing at the front to approximately 6 inches (15 cm) along the sides and back. For a spring front, 6 inches (15 cm) or more might be needed at the front corners and along the ends, maintaining about 6 inches (15 cm) for the back. The same allowance should be added to both sections involved, for example the inner arm and deck at the sides.

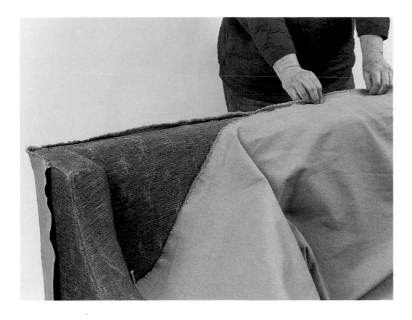

Fabric for the outer back is railroaded. Since laundering the fabric caused no puckering along the selvage, it is left intact and placed along the upper edge. Normally the selvages should be cut off, or at least clipped at frequent intervals. At this edge just seam allowance is added, with the upholstery seam as a guide to seamline placement for the cover piece.

A skirt will be added at the lower edge. The fabric is heavy enough to hang well without being attached at the lower edge, so it is cut just to the skirt placement line plus the width of the seam allowance.

The outer and inner back pieces are pinned along the upper back seamline.

6. Cut the deck.

This piece should equal the inner back in length. It can be pinned along the lower edge of the inner back now. The outer edge should correspond to the seam at which platform cloth is sewn to the front upholstery panels.

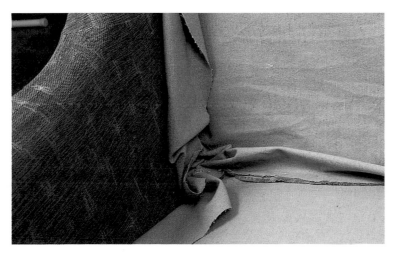

The inner back and deck sections are pinned together. Notice the tuck-in allowance included, the same amount for both pieces.

7. Cut the front sections.

These are cut with the grain running vertically, the seams corresponding to the upholstery. On the end sections, add the same tuck-in allowance that is added to the deck piece.

The square front sections can be pinned together, and to the deck, as they are cut.

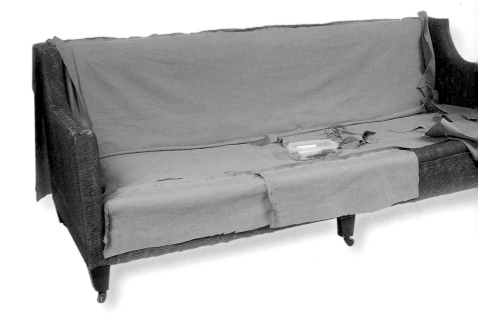

The front sections are trimmed evenly just below the skirt placement line.

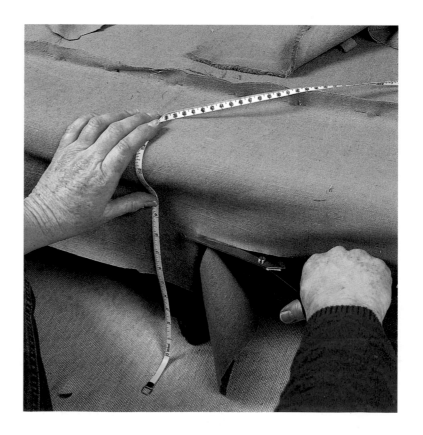

8. Pin darts and front corner seams.

When the cover is pinned wrong side out, be sure to try the cover on the furniture right side out as soon as the darts are sewn. There is often a slight variance between two corners that appear identical, and a slight adjustment may be necessary.

The excess is trimmed away at the front corner seam. The lower end of the dart seam will be slightly above the seamline joining the deck tuck-in to the inner arm tuck-in as shown in the drawing on page 70.

A deep tuck-in allowance was added for this spring-edge couch.

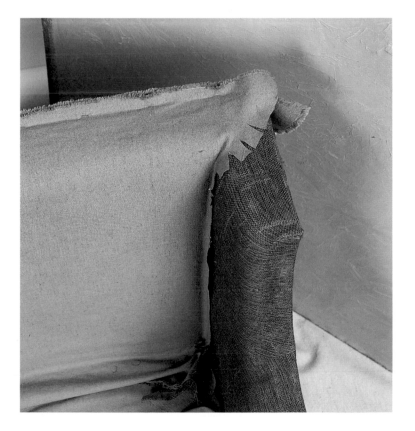

9. Fit the inner back to the inner arm.

Determine where the seamline will be. In this case, the cover will follow the upholstery seam. Trim to leave ½ inch (1.5 cm) seam allowance, or the width you prefer.

Clip from the edge nearly to the seamline to eliminate puckering and assure a neat fit around the curve of the inner back/inner arm seam. The upper part of this seam is on the bias grain which also will contribute to a smooth fit.

10. Fit the upper section of the inner arm.

This area is treated as a modified wing. The inner arm is cut as two pieces to provide a seam at the "crook" of the arm for fitting. The seam between the two is dictated by the upholstery seamline. Cut both inner arm sections with the lengthwise fabric grain perpendicular to the floor, regardless of the slope of the arm.

With the inner back in place, the corresponding edge of the inner wing section can be pin-fitted. The seam allowance is clipped to accommodate the curve of the seamline.

11. Pin darts at corners.

A dart gives shape to the upper corner. The lower seam is curved, so once again the seam allowance should be clipped.

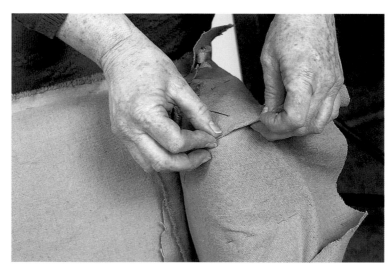

It is rarely necessary to pin the fabric to the upholstery during fitting, but the fitting of this small piece is somewhat critical.

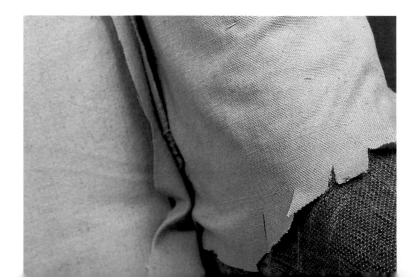

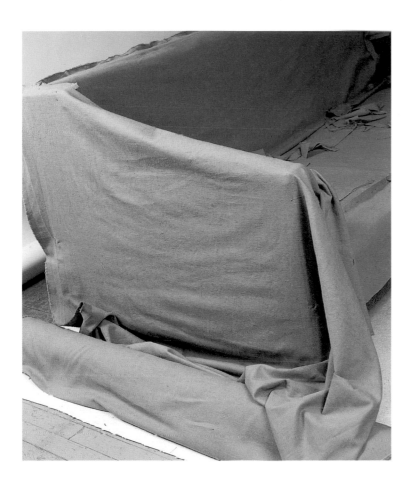

12. Block out the outer arm.

This piece is also cut vertically. Because the use of two separate inner arm pieces took care of fit at the curve, this section can be cut as a single flat piece. The seam will be at the outer edge of the wing and arm. Allow 3 inches (8 cm) at each back corner for the zipper seams. If the corner will not have a zipper, locate the seam just past the corner on the back.

13. Cut the outer arm.

The outer arm section is blocked out, ready to trim and pin. Notice that lengths of fabric are cut from the roll only as they are used.

The outer arm section is in place. The width that remains after this piece is cut can be used for cushion covers or for welt.

The inner arm section is ready to fit.

14. Cut the inner arm.

Block out the lower inner arm section. At the front, allow enough fabric to wrap across the arm front to the arm's outer corner. In length, the piece must be long enough to include a tuck-in allowance equal to that of the deck end. At the front of the arm, the lower edge should be just below the skirt line.

The tuck-in allowance at the lower edge of the inner arm section corresponds to that added at the end of the deck.

15. Fit the arm and wing sections.

Fit the inner arm to the inner back and to the lower edge of the wing. Now the wing/outer arm seam can be pinned. Then continue pinning down the arm, fitting the inner/outer arm seam. Pin the back corner seam that will not have a zipper.

At the arm front, bring the end of the inner arm piece around the front of the arm and fit to the outer arm section down the corner. Pin a dart in the inner arm piece at the top of the arm.

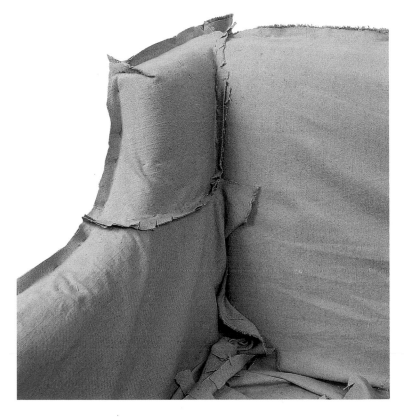

Work from the back of the inner arm section to the front, fitting and pinning to the corresponding sections.

There is no sewing mishap that can't be corrected with a little creative thinking! We could add a patch, or a secret pocket…or simply make the skirt an inch or so longer than planned.

16. Cut the skirt.

A skirt can take any form that appeals to you: ruffled or pleated, long or short. A traditional skirt is straight around the piece with an inverted pleat at each corner. The fashion in skirt lengths for furniture changes just as it does for women. Experiment to see what looks best with the style of your chair. The skirt should be cut with the same fabric grain orientation as the outer cover sections.

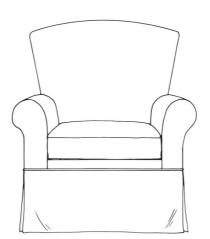
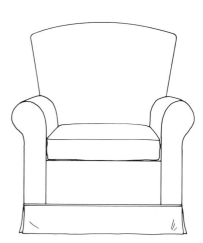

For the traditional skirt as shown on the couch slipcover, allow for a pleat depth of 4 inches (10 cm). To the skirt circumference measurement, add twice the pleat depth for each pleat. To accommodate the zipper opening, add the same allowance at the side and back as is added to those cover pieces. Locate piecing seams inside the pleats.

The slipcover is on the couch and in service. The skirt length is just right.

A skirt will hang better if it is lined. For lighter weight fabrics, simply double the skirt length to cut the fabric. Use lighter weight lining with heavier fabrics and cut it the size of the skirt. Add seam allowance at the sides of each piece and at the upper edge.

Fit the skirt with the cover pinned and in place. Construct the skirt as described on page 70. Match the basting line at the skirt upper edge to the cover placement line. At the zipper seam, match raw edges. Pin in the corner pleats, omitting a pleat on the back at a corner or corners where a zipper will be located.

VARIATIONS FOR A CHAIR

Several generations have relaxed in this treasured old chair. The wide rolled arms and thick seat and back cushions give it a comfort factor that makes it well worth re-covering.

The chosen fabric, however, presents a real challenge. The pattern is an irregular stripe with no discernable repeat. Even with the extra fabric that was purchased, there was no way to match stripes at every seamline.

The best solution is to arrange such a fabric in a way that pleases the eye. Here, the idea is to center a dominant stripe at the center back. Pattern matching is most noticeable up the front and inner back, and on the seat cushion. There was adequate fabric to match the deck section as well. Remember that pinning the cover wrong side out means that the pattern will read in the opposite direction on the finished cover.

The arms are set back from the front, so the front cover section wraps around at the front corner to meet the outer arm seam. Because the chair has a firm front edge rather than a spring edge, no breakaway allowance is needed. A 3-inch (8-cm) tuck-in allowance is added at the sides of the deck section. The front section has the same amount of tuck-in added toward the back, where it is sewn to the deck, but this tapers around the arm to a standard seam allowance at the outer arm seam.

A slipcover, by definition, won't have the close fit of upholstery. The horizontal inner/outer arm seam will be raised slightly, resulting in a slighter degree of roll over the arm and a looser fit down the side. The new seamline is chalk marked on the chair arm to fit the cover.

The small, intricate tucks used to shape the front of the inner arm are converted, for a looser cover, to three larger tucks. Folds of tucks like these usually are downward; when the cover is pinned wrong side out, fold them upward.

Assembling the Cover

The sewing will go much better if the machine is set up on a table large enough to accommodate this large quantity of fabric. If the machine's feed mechanism has to pull against the weight of fabric hanging off the edge of the table, uneven stitches and broken needles will be the result.

Use a larger machine needle than for everyday sewing. With heavily finished fabric, such as polished cotton, use a sharp-pointed needle rather than the standard universal point. If you are sewing with a softer cotton or cotton blend, clean the lint from the bobbin area regularly.

Study the pinned cover before removing it from the furniture. You should be quite familiar with its construction by now, and have a good idea of how it will be sewn. The following guidelines are generic; your cover may have additional or fewer seams.

1. Sew the welt. Detailed instructions for making and attaching welt are on page 17.

   Where welt will be added to a seam, unpin the seam a section at a time and put the welt in place. Sew with a piping or zipper foot.

2. Stitch any darts, sewing from the fabric edge toward the point and shortening the stitch length at the narrow end.

3. Sew the deck section to the inner arms and inner back. Stitch seams at the front breakaway point as shown.

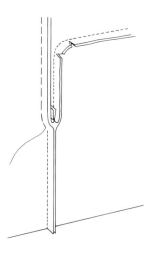

4. Sew each inner arm/inner wing seam, if applicable.

5. Sew inner arm/wing pieces to the inner back.

6. Sew the inner and outer arm seams.

7. Sew front arm panels in place.

8. Sew the outer arm to the outer back at the seam without the zipper.

9. Sew the inner back to the outer back, leaving approximately 8 inches (20 cm) open at the zipper area.

10. If a skirt will be added, attach it before installing the zipper.

    • For a doubled skirt, fold the piece right side out along the lower edge and baste the upper raw edges together.

    • For a lined skirt, sew the skirt to the lining with right sides together just along the lower edge. If the cover fabric is very heavy, understitch: stitch the lining to the seam allowances approximately $\frac{1}{4}$ inch (.5 cm) from the seamline. Turn, press, and baste the upper raw edges together.

    • For a seam with welt, end the welting $\frac{3}{4}$ inch (2 cm) from the end of the skirt at the zipper opening on the outer arm section, and 2 inches (5 cm) from the end on the cover back.

    • With right sides together, pin the skirt to the cover, lower edge upward, the basting stitching aligned with the placement line. Stitch.

11. Install the zipper. Use a heavy-duty zipper made especially for slipcovers; these can be bought by the yard. Buy a length slightly longer than the length (height) of the cover back.

    • At each back/outer arm seamline that was left open, turn $\frac{3}{4}$ inch (2 cm) to the wrong side along each edge; press.

- Close the zipper and place it right side up against the wrong side of one pressed edge. Position it with the pull at the lower edge of the cover.

- Align the fabric fold at the center of the teeth and stitch to approximately 1 inch (2.5 cm) from the lower edge.

- If the zipper ends are unfinished, stitch securely by hand over the last teeth at the upper end using heavy thread. At the lower hemline, turn under the ends and whipstitch in place.

- At the upper end, fold a pleat in the back section to cover the zipper seam. Match the outer and inner back seamlines for fit. Press the pleat lightly.

- On the inside, stitch along the inner pleat, stitching close to the fold through the two thicknesses. Viewed from the upper edge, the zipper area will resemble the drawing.

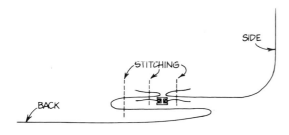

12. Stitch the remaining part of the upper back seam.

13. Hem the lower edge, or finish it with a casing to tie under the chair or couch.

- With the cover in place, fold under the lower edge around each leg and finger press, or pin along the foldline.

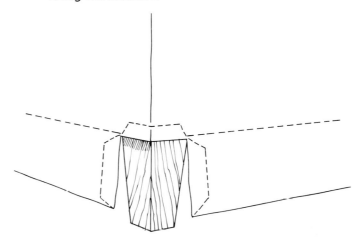

- Staystitch the foldline and clip to the stitching so the fabric lies smoothly. Edgestitch around each curve, or trim and clean-finish the seam allowances.

- On each of the four sides, fold a double hem to form a casing. Beginning at the zipper seam, or at one leg, thread a strong cord through the casing.

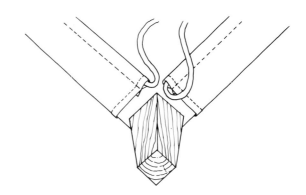

6 ▪ Tailored Slipcover Projects

The more fitted slipcovers shown on these pages exhibit a wonderful variety of shapes and styles. Some are very simple and fairly quick to make; others are more detailed. All of them can be cut and fitted according to the steps illustrated in the preceding chapter.

FLORAL SLIPCOVER

Fresh summer flowers and a cool blue background combine to cover a comfortable chair. This cover fits closely and is cut to make the most of the all-over print.

Instructions for upholstering the ottomon are on page 00.

The careful fit gives the cover a very neat appearance. The design was planned with simple, clean lines to let the fabric's print show to its best advantage. There are minimal seams, and there is no welt.

The cover is cut with the outer and inner arm as a single piece so that there is no break in the pattern. The fit of the arm results from the shaping of the separate front arm panel. There are openings at both back corners, otherwise so fitted a cover would be difficult to remove.

The lower edge of the cover is approximately 1 inch (2.5 cm) below the bottom of the chair and is finished with a blind hem.

The cover for the T-shaped back cushion can be made by tracing around the seamlines of the existing cover. This one has a zipper in the boxing strip that extends across the lower edge and for approximately 2 inches (5 cm) up each side. Detailed instructions for box cushions are on page 27.

To make the cover, follow the instructions that begin on page 53, but with these changes:

1. Cut the inner and outer arm as one piece. For a directional pattern, cut the piece so that the pattern is the right way up on the outer arm.

2. At the back corners, add 3 inches (8 cm) to all pieces that meet at these points. For this chair,

the inner back, outer back, and arm pieces are affected.

3. On the back piece, hem the edges to this measurement and overlap the arm and inner back pieces. Stitch a narrow hem along the underlay.

4. Hook and loop tape closures are used here to maintain the simplicity of the design, spaced evenly from the top of the chair to the point just below the arm. With a plain fabric, decorative buttons or ties could be added as a design feature. For lightweight fabric, it is a good idea to press a strip of fusible interfacing to the wrong side of each hem allowance.

BUTTONED SLIPCOVER

It is details that change an average design to one that is extraordinary. On this stylish cover, bound buttonholes and covered buttons accent the back pleat. Contrasting welt defines the upper arm gusset, and a very short skirt of the same fabric accents the lower edge.

Careful placement of so large a pattern makes all the difference in a fitted cover. Here, the pattern is centered on the outer arms and on each half of the back. Stripes match at the upper back seam and at the inner back/seat seam. The fabric is a medium weight linen and cotton blend, just right for the tailored look of the cover.

MEASURING AND CUTTING

Cut, fit, and pin the cover wrong side out following the steps illustrated in Chapter 5 with the changes listed below.

1. Plan the lower edge of the main cover to reach about 1 inch (2.5 cm) below the bottom of the chair.

2. On the outer back, add a Quick Box Pleat as described on page 40. Work bound buttonholes along the pleat. Instructions are on page 77.

3. For a wide arm like this one, cut separate gusset strips for the upper arms. The strips extend from the upper back seam to the lower edge of the main cover. The upper back corner of the inner arm tapers to a point where the gusset joins the inner back.

4. The seat and front are a single piece.

5. Add tuck-in allowance, if needed, at the seat sides and back and at the lower edges of the inner back and inner arms.

6. The skirt sections are doubled fabric, with the fold at the lower edge. The side/back sections extend from the front corners to the pleat folds at center back. The third section is corner to corner across the front. Seam allowances at the ends of each piece are pressed to the inside.

7. Welt is sewn into both sides of each arm gusset seam, and into the skirt seam at the lower edge.

CONSTRUCTION

1. Make the welt. Detailed instructions for making and attaching welt are on page 17.

2. Follow the construction steps on page 70, incorporating welt into the gusset seams.

3. Stitch welt around the lower edge, aligning the corded edge of the welt with the seamline. Begin and end the welt at the center back pleat folds.

4. Sew the skirt sections in place, stitching just next to the welt stitching line.

5. Cover large buttons with fabric scraps and sew in place inside the back pleat.

6. Fold under the ends of each skirt section and fold in half lengthwise, right side out. Press.

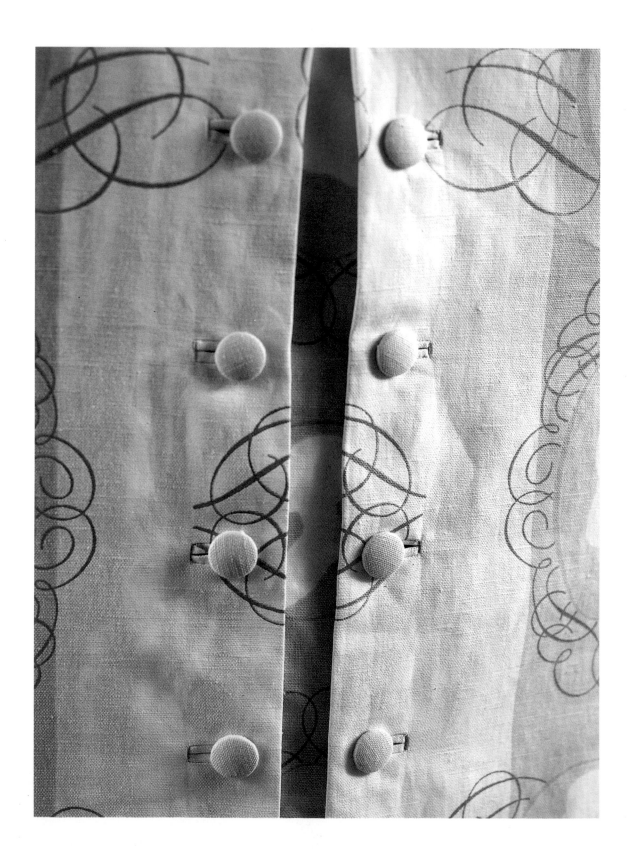

BOUND BUTTONHOLES

Bound, or welt, buttonholes add the same beautiful accent to slipcovers as to designer garments. The version illustrated here is not difficult to make and is very nearly foolproof. Try a sample with a scrap of your cover fabric before working on the cover itself.

1. For lightweight or unstable fabrics, fuse a strip of very lightweight interfacing along the wrong side of the buttonhole area.

2. Mark buttonhole positions on the wrong side of the outer back along the center pleat. Place the upper buttonhole at least 6 inches (15 cm) below the upper seamline. The inner ends of the buttonholes should be ½ inch (1.3 cm) from the center back crease of the pleat. The length of each buttonhole should equal the diameter plus twice the thickness of the button. Mark each end of each buttonhole.

3. For welt for each buttonhole, cut a bias strip of fabric 2 inches wide and 1½ inches (4 cm) longer than the finished buttonhole length.

4. Fuse a strip of lightest weight tricot interfacing to the wrong side of each welt strip.

5. Fold the long edges of the strip to the wrong side so they meet precisely at the center and so that both halves are equal in width.

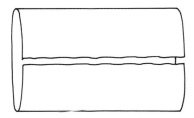

6. On the wrong side of the cover back, center a folded strip over the buttonhole markings, cut edges up.

7. Carefully mark the ends of the buttonhole, marking across the full width of the strip.

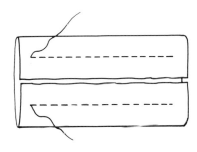

8. Stitch between the end markings on each half of the strip, stitching precisely halfway between the cut edge and the fold, and beginning and ending the stitching precisely at the marked lines. Do not backstitch, but begin and end the stitching line with a very short stitch length.

9. Cutting along the center line of the welt, cut through all layers to ½ inch (1.3 cm) from each end. Then clip carefully into each corner.

10. Turn the welts to the right side.

11. On the wrong side, fold back the triangular ends squarely at the ends of the buttonhole. Press.

12. Stitch across each triangular section along the foldline. Begin and end the stitching just at the corners. Reverse sewing direction several times so the ends are stitched securely.

13. Press the center back pleat folds neatly. Hand baste around each buttonhole through both the outer back and pleat facing layers, stitching ¾ inch (2 cm) from the buttonhole itself.

14. Mark each end of the buttonhole opening on the facing side by pushing a pin straight through both layers from the outside.

15. On the facing side, carefully cut a slit through only the facing layer from one pin to the other.

16. Turn the raw edges to the inside and hand stitch the folds to the back of the welts..

A ROOM FOR A SUMMER COTTAGE

*T*he room's subtle shades invoke images of the seashore—a pale, hazy sky, sand and driftwood, whitecaps on the waves. Slipcovers for the chairs, linen and cotton fabric without a hint of color, are cut with the simplest possible lines. The couch cover is sleek and understated, trimmed with linen welt to echo the wood tones of the room.

Instructions for the ottoman cover are on page 45.

WHITE CHAIR COVERS

A close fit around the arms accentuates the unusual shape of the chairs. Separate gussets along the upper arms end in pleats at the skirt front and back seamlines.

CUTTING AND FITTING

Block in the cover pieces and pin the seams, wrong side out, on the chair following the illustrated steps that begin on page 56.

Note the following construction details when cutting the cover.

1. This chair has a firm front edge and seat, so minimal tuck-in allowance is needed around the seat. The firm edge also allows a high skirt placement line. The skirt seamline is at the front edge.

2. The inner back extends around the sides to the back corners and across the upper back. The upper corners are fitted with darts.

3. The skirt front and back pieces are cut with 4-inch (10-cm) pleat extensions at each side. An extension of the same width is added at the front and back of each skirt side section to form the pleat underlays.

CONSTRUCTION

Follow the construction steps on page 70, with these changes:

1. Incorporate the gussets in the inner/outer arm seams.

2. To make the skirt, first stitch the lengthwise seams of the pleat extensions at each corner.

3. Stitch the pleat closed several inches from the skirt upper edge along the corner.

4. Fold the extensions toward center front and center back and baste across the upper edges.

STRIPED COUCH COVER

With construction details kept to a minimum, the bold pattern of the fabric looks its best. The stripes are matched to perfection at the front seam and where the seat joins the inner back. On the front arm panels the stripes are perfectly vertical, emphasizing the graceful outward curve of the arms.

The natural linen not only provides a pleasant color contrast to the cover fabric, it is also practical. Because of its durability, linen is the ideal fabric to use along edges that are subject to the hardest wear.

MAKING THE COVER

The cover is blocked out and pinned on the couch as illustrated in the instructions beginning on page 56. Note the following construction details when planning the cover:

1. The front/deck seam is located at the break-away point.

2. The inner back and arms extend across the top to the outer back edges.

3. The outer back, outer arms, front arm panels, and front all extend to the lower edge.

4. There is no skirt, nor any pleats at the lower edge. Instead it is trimmed with welt.

CONTRASTS IN BLUE AND WHITE

*F*urnishings in blue and white are a perfect complement to the room's wood tones. *The atmosphere is cool and relaxing, a comfortable place to share with friends or to enjoy a quiet evening.*

Instructions for the upholstered table are on page 131.

CHAIR COVERS

Two identical chairs take on separate personalities with new covers in contrasting patterns.

MAKING THE COVER

Follow the instructions that begin on page 56 to fit and sew the cover. Instructions for making and applying welt are on page 17.

Note the following construction details:

1. The inner back extends over the top to the outer back seam just below the roll.

2. The inner arm extends over the arm in the same way, with the outer arm seam placed just below the roll.

3. A separate shoulder panel is sewn between the inner and outer back sections above the arm. Welt is included in the seam from the arm in front, up over the back, to the lower edge. At the lower end of the shoulder, seam allowances are turned under and edgestitched to the inner arm.

4. Separate front arm panels are trimmed with welt from the breakaway point at the deck seam around to the lower edge at the front corner. Below the breakaway, a pleat underlay extension is added to the panel.

5. Pleat extensions also are added at the sides of the front panel. The arm and front extensions are sewn together with a vertical seam, then folded toward center front to form the pleat.

6. The cushion cover is made as described on page 27. Welt is sewn into the seams.

WHITE LOVE SEAT

Construction of the love seat cover is identical to that of the chairs; it is simply wider. Because the fabric is a solid color and very stable, it can be railroaded, eliminating the need for seams on the front and back.

The matching accent pillow on the couch can be made according to the instructions for the knife-edge pillow, page 26.

COUNTRY REDS

*R*ich tones of red impart casual warmth to the room. The variety of fabrics
and textures adds up to a comfortable and cheerful place to relax.

THE COUCH

Thick cotton jacquard is a good slipcover fabric. It is easy to work with, resists wrinkles, and has enough body that the cover will hang attractively. This cover is made according to the instructions shown in Chapter 5. It has fewer pieces; the upper arms extend to the height of the back. Welt trims the outer edges and the skirt seamline.

TIED PILLOW

The pillow resting against the end of the couch is made from a simple design, with ties at one end instead of a zipper.

1. Cut fabric for the pillow front and back, using the pillow dimensions plus seam allowance at all sides.

2. Cut two strips for facing, each 7 inches (18 cm) wide and the length of one side of the pillow.

3. Make four ties approximately 10 inches (26 cm) long and finished at one end, or use lengths of ribbon.

4. Stitch the ends of the facing strips with right sides together. Hem one long edge.

5. Stitch pillow cover sections, right sides together, around three sides.

6. Pin unfinished ends of the ties to the cover right side, two on the front and two opposite them on the back.

7. Pin the facing to the cover, right sides together, aligning raw edges. Stitch, keeping the ties free.

CUSHION-TOPPED OTTOMAN

An attached top cushion adds height, so the ottoman works as a table just as well.

MEASURING AND CUTTING

Add ½ inch (1.5 cm) where seam allowances are indicated.

1. For the cushion top, measure the cushion width and length. Add seam allowance at all sides

and cut the piece. Round the corners as necessary to match the cushion.

2. For the underside of the cushion, cut two pieces equal in length to the length of the cushion top piece, and 3½ inches (9 cm) wide. Cut two pieces equal in length to the width of the cushion top, and 3½ inches (9 cm) wide.

3. For the cushion side, cut a strip equal in length to twice the combined length and width of the cushion top piece. In width, cut it the cushion thickness plus double the seam allowance.

4. For the ottoman, measure the circumference around the top and add twice the seam allowance. This will be the cutting width.

5. For the length, determine the desired finished length, add hem allowance, and add 3 inches (8 cm). Cut fabric to these measurements.

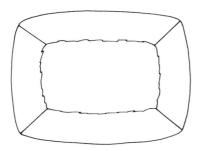

6. Cut the skirt, allowing for a self facing, according to the instructions on page 70.

7. Cut strips for welt around the cushion upper and lower edges and above the skirt. Instructions for making welt are on page 17.

CONSTRUCTION

1. Make the cushion cover. Stitch the ends of the edge strip together. With the seam at one corner, mark the other corner positions on the seamline of each long edge, using the cover top as a guide.

2. Stitch welt around the cushion top and to the lower edge of the edge strip (see page 19).

3. Stitch a cover underside section to each side of the edge strip lower edge, ending the stitching at each corner seamline.

4. Place this piece on the cushion, wrong side out. Pin a diagonal seam at each corner to miter the corners. Remove the cover and stitch the seams.

5. Stitch the cover top to the edge strip, matching corners.

6. Make the ottoman cover. Stitch the ends with right sides together.

7. Hem the lower edge.

8. Make and attach the skirt according to the instructions on page 70.

9. Place the cover on the ottoman, wrong side out. Pin a dart at each corner to miter the corners. The width of the border around the top should equal the width of the cushion underside pieces.

10. Remove the cover and stitch the darts.

11. With right sides together, pin the cushion cover underside to the ottoman top around the inner raw edges. Stitch.

12. Put the cushion into its cover, and the cover over the ottoman.

SLIPCOVER WITH PLEATED SKIRT

As fresh and pretty as springtime, a floral print like this one lends a distinctly feminine quality to the room. The box pleated skirt adds a tailored touch to balance the overall look of the cover.

Several features of this cover design add up to big savings in construction time: Ties, rather than zippers, close the back corner openings. And instead of a separate cushion cover, the cushion is covered as if it were part of the chair. There is no inner/outer arm seam. Instead, the two are cut as a single piece. This time-saver also is the best method to use with a pattern like this one as it eliminates the need to interrupt the pattern with a seam at a conspicuous point.

MAKING THE COVER

Pin and construct the cover according to the illustrated slipcover instructions that begin on page 53. This cover will differ in the following ways:

1. The inner back extends across the upper back.

2. A separate shoulder panel is sewn between the inner and outer back sections.

3. The seat and front are made up of a single piece of fabric. Because the seat section covers the chair cushion, very deep tuck-in allowances must be added at the sides and back of the seat, and at the lower edges of the inner back and inner arms.

4. Separate arm panels extend to the skirt seam on each side of the front.

5. At the back corners, add 6 inches (15 cm) to each side of the back and to the shoulder panel and outer arm. Before the upper back seam is sewn, hem all four extensions. Fold under the back extensions just inside the back corners, press the folds, and topstitch along them. Lap the back over the side extensions at the upper edge when the upper back seam is sewn. Sew ties to the facing side of the back, and to the side extensions.

6. Make a box pleated skirt. Except for a half pleat at each edge, there are no pleats across the back.

• Plan the pleats in order to calculate the total skirt width. Allow 3 to 4 inches (8 to 10 cm) for the pleat depth. Add four times the pleat depth for each box pleat, and twice the pleat depth for each corner half pleat.

• Where piecing seams are necessary, try to hide them inside pleats. Include piecing seam allowances in the total width calculation.

• The pleated skirt will resemble the illustration. Use the diagram to calculate the total skirt width that will be needed.

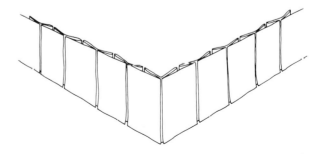

• Form the pleats and baste them across the upper edge before sewing the skirt to the cover.

QUICK TIED COVER

The fabric is a homey cotton plaid, easy to sew and with just the right look for this simple slipcover design. A single piece makes up the seat and front and covers the cushion as if it were part of the chair. Ties shape the front corners, and close the openings at back corners.

Destined for quick construction, this cover combines pieces, meaning fewer seams to sew. Ties replace the back zippers. With the cushion under the main cover, there is no separate cushion cover to make. The photograph shows self ties at the back openings and front gussets. To save time, use purchased ribbon for the ties.

MAKING THE COVER

Pin and construct the cover according to the illustrated slipcover instructions beginning on page 53. This cover has several different construction features.

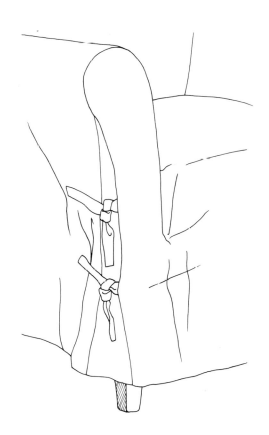

1. The inner back extends across the upper back edge.

2. A shoulder panel is sewn between the inner and outer back sections, and to the arm at the lower edge.

3. The inner and outer arm sections are cut as a single piece.

4. Separate front arm panels are sewn at their inner edges to the lower front.

5. A gusset is installed between the outer edge of the arm panel and the outer arm. It is 3 inches (8 cm) wide at the hemline and tapers to nothing just below the arm roll. Ties are sewn into both sides of the gusset seam.

6. The single seat/front piece has a dart on each side that is sewn from the breakaway point to the cushion corner.

7. At the back, add a 6-inch (15-cm) extension to the shoulder and outer arm to form an underlay at each back opening. Add the same amount to each side of the outer back.

Hem all four extensions. Fold under the back extensions just inside the back corners, press the folds, and topstitch along them. Lap the back over the side extensions at the upper edge to sew the upper back seam. Sew ties to the facing side of the back, and to the side extensions.

SLIPCOVER WITH AN APRON

*W*hen a chair is placed with its back to the doorway, it's fun to add styling details to the slipcover back. On this one, the arm covering panels extend to the back of the chair where they are tied like a chef's apron.

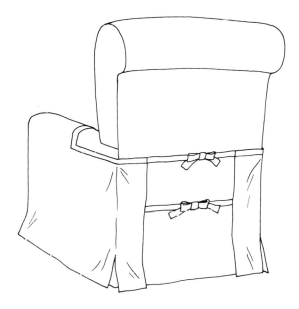

The cover can be cut and fitted as illustrated in Chapter 5. Note these differences in the design of this cover.

1. All of the outer panels extend almost to the floor. At the front corners are vents for ease. Just add wider seam allowances on the outer arm and front arm sections to allow for hems along the openings.

2. A separate shoulder panel is placed at the upper back between the inner and outer back panels. It is fitted to the arm panel at the lower edge.

3. There is not a separate cover for the cushion. A single panel covers the seat and front, and is fitted with the cushion in place in the chair. This means adding a much deeper tuck-in

around the seat and to the inner back and arm sections.

4. The front and back arm panels are each a single piece. Each extends from the tuck-in at the seat over the arm to the hem.

5. There are separate arm front panels.

The fitting sequence for the cover also differs slightly from that illustrated in Chapter 5. The same techniques for pinning and construction apply, though.

1. Fit the outer back, inner back, and shoulder.

2. Fit the back section of the inner/outer arm. Stitch these pieces.

3. Fit the front inner/outer arm and arm front panels. Stitch.

4. Add bindings and ties to the inner/outer arm sections. The back edge of each is bound from the tuck-in at the seat, over the arm, across the outer arm to the end of the piece, then extending to create the ties. The vertical back edges of the piece also are bound. Two additional ties are sewn at the back.

   • For this chair, the binding and tie strips are cut 4 inches (10 cm) wide and finished 1½ inches (4 cm) wide.

   • Bind the vertical back edges of the arm sections first. Fold and press each binding strip in half, right side out, along the length. Sew with binding right side to cover right side. Fold strip to the cover wrong side and fold under the seam allowance so the fold just covers the previous stitching line. Stitch from the right side along the previous stitching line.

   • For the upper edge of the arm, sew binding in the same way, starting at the inner arm tuck-in. Miter the corner at the outer arm, continuing the stitching along the ties.

   • Make the two separate ties and sew them in place on the back edges.

5. Fit the front arm pieces over the rear arms and back. Stitch together along the tuck-in, and stitch the seat/front in place.

7 ▪ Quick Upholstery

Reupholstering a drop-in chair seat or a footstool is a rewarding experience that provides instant gratification. Such a project also offers the opportunity to learn upholstery techniques and become familiar with the use of the tools and materials without committing a great deal of time or spending a fortune for materials.

If your home can't provide a shabby candidate for an experimental project of this kind, it is always possible to find one at a flea market or charity shop. Some people would never consider taking on a re-covering job and would give away a perfectly good piece of furniture instead.

CHOOSING FABRIC

Nearly any fabric can be used to cover a chair seat. Firmly woven, medium to fairly heavy cotton and cotton blend fabrics work well. Heavy weight fabrics can last longer, but be sure the fabric isn't so thick that it will prevent the chair seat fitting into the chair.

If your heart's desire is a fabric that is light in weight or loosely woven, or one that stretches, use a firm fabric or a firmly woven interfacing underneath for body. Consider machine quilting the surface to hold the two together.

Chair seats and small stools offer a practical way to display a piece of needlework or a special piece of fabric. There are great bargains to be found in remnants that are too small to use for much else, but plenty large enough to cover the seat of a chair.

To figure the amount of fabric to buy, measure the width and depth of the chair seat and add about 6 inches (15 cm) each direction. If a piece of fabric that you particularly want to use is smaller than this, but large enough to cover the visible area of the chair, you can sew on a margin of some other material. Use a sturdy fabric. Overlap the edges of the two and sew them together with two rows of zigzag stitch.

REUPHOLSTERING A DROP-IN CHAIR SEAT

A drop-in, or loose, seat refers to the style usually found on straight chairs such as dining chairs, kitchen chairs, or that seldom-used chair in the corner of the living room. Replacing the cover on such a chair is a short evening's work, new padding included.

The materials and tools needed for this job are few. Some of the upholsterer's tools shown in Chapter 2 are very helpful. What you need will depend upon the construction of your chair. Take out the seat to see how it is put together.

1. Remove the seat from the chair

Usually it is held in place with screws on the under-side. Sometimes it is attached from the upper side, the screws then covered with decorative trim that is stapled in place.

2. Remove the old covering and padding

Take off the bottom dust cover to get to the works of the chair. Removing the old upholstery is a matter of pulling out hundreds of staples or tacks. An upholsterer's staple remover, an inexpensive tool, is worth its weight in gold about the time you have removed about a dozen staples (or parts of them) the hard way and bloodied your fingers in the process. Likewise, the ripping chisel or claw tool for prying out tacks that have been hammered in by someone's personal trainer. A tap on the tool's handle with a mallet is the easier way to accomplish the job.

Remove every broken staple. These become lethal weapons when you attach the new covering, so pull them all out with pliers. Any remaining shards that can't be budged should be tapped in flush with the wood with a tack hammer.

Throw away the old tacks. Those that aren't bent will have dull points. New tacks are inexpensive and much easier to use.

By the time a chair needs a new covering, its padding may be in need of replacement too. What is the point of a fine new cover if the chair still looks tired and saggy? A foam cushion can be re-used as long as it still has its shape and has not begun to disintegrate. Curled hair or coir, commonly used in older furniture, lose their spring after a time and should be replaced. Battings, too, become compacted and hard. Fillings of feathers and down sometimes can be resuscitated by a dry cleaner who specializes in that process.

If your chair has a plywood seat rather than webbing, check whether the frame is such that webbing could be used instead. Webbing makes the chair more comfortable.

Webbing is available where upholstery fabrics and materials are sold. An inexpensive webbing stretcher is a necessary tool; it is difficult to pull the strips tight enough without this aid.

Generally, if the chair is well made, it is a good idea to attach the new webbing in the same pattern as the old. Webbing strips usually are interwoven, with 1 to 1½ inches (2.5 to 4 cm) space between.

Use a heavy-duty or upholstery stapler, or use tacks to attach the webbing. Working on the bottom of the frame, attach strips across the depth of the seat first. Work from the roll of webbing, cutting it as you go.

Double the end of the strip and tack or staple it in place. Use four or five tacks, placing them in an irregular pattern. Stretch the strip tightly across the frame and secure it with a couple of tacks. It should be tight enough to support weight, but not so tight that it will break. Leave 1 to 1½ inches (2.5 to 4 cm) excess and cut the strip. Fold the end over and tack or staple it securely. Interweave the crosswise strips and attach them in the same way.

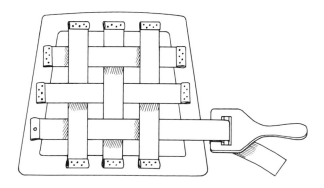

4. Replace the burlap

Burlap supports the seat cushion or filling. It, too, loses its resiliency over the years.

Cut the new piece with a good margin around the edges. Pull it taut across the frame and keep it in place with a few tacks or staples. Fold over the edge of the fabric and tack it securely through the double fabric thickness. Trim off the excess.

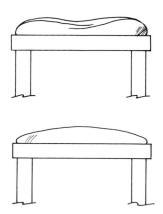

3. Replace the webbing

Most straight chairs have a base of burlap webbing to support the seat padding or cushion. This material also loses its resiliency in time. It is not difficult to replace it, and the time it takes to do the job is worth investing.

5. Replace the padding or cushion

Generally, the results are most predictable if the seating is replaced with the same kind of materials as were removed. If the chair is very old, or was not well made, you can improve upon the original and make the chair more comfortable.

To replace a foam cushion, use high-density foam that is meant for seating. Foam pillow forms are too soft for this purpose. Upholstery suppliers can cut foam to your size specifications.

A moderately thin layer of cotton or polyester batting over the foam will improve the looks and comfort of the seat. Cut it just to the edges of the frame so it won't interfere with the fit of the seat. With a plywood seat the foam should be glued in place with foam adhesive to keep it from slipping.

Curled hair or coir should be arranged on the burlap in a dome shape. Press it in place firmly, and keep it from draping over the edges of the frame. The pros sew the fiber in place, using heavy thread and long, loose stitches. Add a layer of moderately thin batting over the fiber to help shape it and to prevent the fibers from working their way out through the covering.

Old cotton padding might be replaced at least in part with upholstery grade polyester batting, which won't compress as quickly. Use cotton for the under layer and the polyester on top. Cut the material just short of the frame edges so it won't overhang when the cover is in place.

6. Add a muslin cover

Muslin holds the padding in place and helps shape the seat. With a foam cushion, a muslin cover helps taper the edges so the seat won't have a boxy look.

Cut a piece of inexpensive muslin large enough to cover the padding and reach well under the edges of the frame. Pull the muslin firmly over the padding and staple or tack it under the frame. Place one or two tacks at each side, then tack between those tacks and the corners. Secure the corners next. Keep checking the top of the seat to make sure the cover is evenly taut.

Place tacks close together all the way around the frame, keeping the fabric smooth over the corners especially. Try to avoid multiple fabric thickness at

the edge of the frame that might interfere with the seat fitting into the chair.

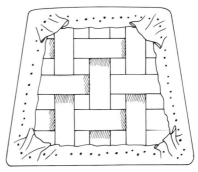

Rearrange the padding as necessary so it is domed at the center and isn't slipping over the edges of the frame. With the muslin in place, the seat should have its finished shape. If loose filling was used, a stuffing regulator can be used to rearrange it within the cover. A large hatpin, upholstery pin, or icepick makes a passable substitute for this tool, although the latter will leave holes in the fabric.

7. Put on the new cover

With the muslin cover smooth and firmly in place, the final cover is a breeze. The fabric should be placed with the lengthwise grain—the direction of least stretch—along the depth of the seat. If the fabric has a nap, like velvet, the nap direction should be toward the front of the chair.

Attach the cover as you did the muslin. Make sure there are no fabric folds at the frame edges that will prevent it fitting into the chair.

Apply a finish to give the cover stain and soil resistance, if desired. Always test the product on a fabric scrap to make sure it won't discolor the fabric or react adversely with the dyes or finishes on the fabric.

8. Add a dust cover

A dust cover renders the work invisible from the underside and keeps the chair clean underneath. Dust cover fabric is available from upholstery suppliers, or tightly woven cotton cambric can be used. On some chairs, a piece of fiberboard or stiff cardboard is used for this purpose.

Attach the dust cover to the bottom of the seat frame as the original cover was. Tack or staple it in such a way that the tacks don't interfere with the fit of the seat into the chair.

FAST RECOVERY

*T*he single chair next to a telephone table or desk can have a fresh new look in
next to no time at all. A drop-in seat like the one on this chair is an opportunity
for instant redecorating. It is a good way to try a new color, to show off a piece of
needlepoint, or to use a pretty remnant that's too small for much of anything else.

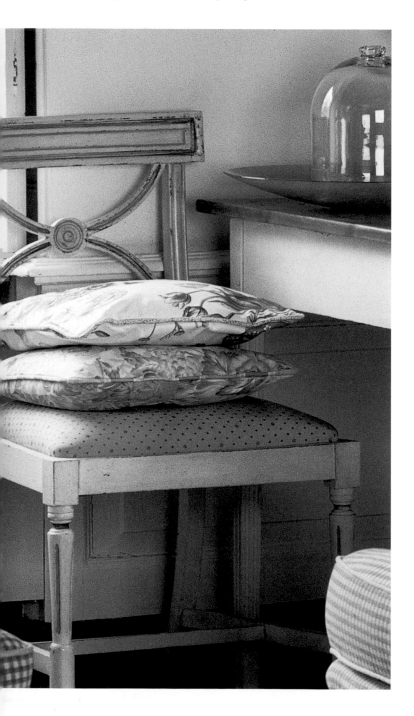

Look the chair over to see how it's put together.
When you take the seat out and the coverings
off, make note of the way it was assembled
so you will be able to get it back together in
the same order. Follow the detailed instructions
for refurbishing and covering the seat that begin
on page 91.

MATERIALS AND TOOLS

Every chair is made up of a different combination of materials. The supplies and tools listed
here may be more or less than you will need for
your own project. Quantities will depend upon
the size of the chair.

    Fabric for cover

    Muslin, for under cover

    Padding or foam for seat

    Burlap square

    Cambric, or dust cover cloth

    Webbing

    Heavy-duty stapler and staples

        or

    Upholstery tacks and tack hammer

CHAIR COVER FROM A REMNANT

A scrap of leftover drapery material or one from a larger reupholstery project can be all you need to refurbish a simple chair. It takes so little time to re-cover a chair like this one that you can do it for any reason—to try out a new color for the next redecorating, to brighten up a dreary corner in the room, or just because it's spring.

Welt, or piping, at the edge of the seat gives the chair professional polish. Purchased welt could be used instead of the self welt shown; it is available where decorator fabrics are sold. Some manufacturers produce welt and other trims that are color-coordinated to their fabrics.

Detailed instructions for making welt can be found on page 17. For this kind of application, the welt will be easier to handle if you cut the bias strips an inch (2.5 cm) or so wider.

Complete instructions for re-covering the chair seat are on page 91. Add the welt after you have put the new cover fabric on the seat. Attach the welt temporarily with a few tacks or staples. Fit the seat onto the chair to check that the welt is in the correct position, then staple it all around.

MATERIALS AND TOOLS

You may not need all the listed supplies for your own project. Read through the instructions to determine the materials you will need.

Fabric for cover

Welt cord or purchased welt

Muslin, for under cover

Padding or foam for seat

Burlap square

Cambric, or dust cover cloth

Webbing

Heavy-duty stapler and staples

    or

Upholstery tacks and tack hammer

MIXED AND MATCHED PATTERNS

A *successful mix of patterns adds visual texture and stops short of busy-ness. A pair of*
chairs that could look quite ordinary are dressed up to become a focal point of the room.

Upholstered backs allow for some enjoyable
experimentation. On these chairs, the upholstered
inner back section fits into a recessed frame just as
the seat does. It is re-covered in almost the same
way. The back is padded with just a layer of batting,
and the muslin under cover is omitted. Use the
original materials as a guide.

Complete instructions for re-covering the seat are
found on page 91. Add welt to the seat and back
after the new cover fabric is in place. Attach the
welt temporarily with a few tacks or staples. Fit the
seat or back onto the chair to check that the welt is
in the correct position, then staple it all around.

MATERIALS AND TOOLS

Supplies will vary with the style and size of the
chair. Read through the instructions to determine
the needs for your project.

Assorted fabric for seat and back covers

Welt trim

Muslin, for under cover

Padding or foam for seat

Burlap square

Cambric, or dust cover cloth

Webbing

Heavy-duty stapler and staples

or

Upholstery tacks and tack hammer

TRIMS FOR CONTRAST

*C*otton fabric with a delicate floral print enhances the chairs' graceful lines. The slightest hint of contrast is added with a bias edging of matching plaid.

The upholstered inner back of the chair is a separate section, fitted into a recessed frame like that of the seat. Corded welt trims the join. For the chair seat, bias-cut welt without the cording was used to avoid a prominent ridge at the point where the seat joins the "show" wood.

MATERIALS AND TOOLS

Supplies will vary with the style and size of the chair. Look at the instructions to determine the needs for your project.

Fabric for seat and back covers

Fabric for contrast welt

Cord for seat back welt

Muslin, for seat under cover

Padding or foam for seat

Burlap square

Cambric, or dust cover cloth

Webbing

Heavy-duty stapler and staples

> or

Upholstery tacks and tack hammer

INSTRUCTIONS

1. Complete instructions for re-covering the seat are found on page 91. The inset back is handled in the same way, padded with a layer of batting and without including the muslin cover.

2. For the back, make corded welt according to the instructions on page 17, using bias-cut fabric strips. Add welt to the back after the new cover fabric is in place. Attach the welt temporarily with a few tacks or staples. Fit the back onto the chair to check that the welt is in the correct position, then staple it all around.

3. For the seat trim, cut bias fabric strips to the required length plus approximately 2 inches (5 cm), and 2½ inches (7 cm) wide. Piece the strips as necessary.

4. Fold the strip in half lengthwise, right side out. Stitch the long edges with ⅝ inch (1.5 cm).

5. Apply the strip to the seat in the same way the back was done, stretching the strip slightly so it conforms to the seat shape. Fold under the end of the strip to overlap the beginning.

HEIRLOOM UPHOLSTERY

A cherished heirloom chair certainly deserves its hand-worked needlepoint cover. If needlepoint is not your forte, purchased fabrics offer a number of less time-consuming and equally elegant options. Woven tapestry, rich brocade, or jewel-toned velvet would produce the same formal effect; heavily textured tussah silk or natural linen could create a more casual look.

Every section of the needlepoint cover was worked to fit, with a plain border of ½ inch (1.5 cm) or so around the patterned area. An additional margin of canvas was allowed when the pieces were cut to shape. Bias-cut strips of lightweight cotton were folded and machine stitched over the edges to prevent fraying.

A chair like this one can be refurbished as described in the instructions on page 91. The cover sections,

instead of being tacked to the underside of the frame, are folded under at the edges and tacked on the outside. Do invest in a new supply of decorative tacks for the job. The points of the old ones will not be sharp enough to penetrate the wood easily.

Use the original materials as a guide for renewing the chair's padding. Read through the instructions and take off the old covering to determine what you will need.

QUICK FOOTSTOOL COVERS

An hour ago, these two footstools were identical. Their design allows for a variety of upholstering options, all of them quick and effortless. The stool in the background was given just a new top covering. On the stool in front, batting and covering were also added to the base.

The footstool is designed so that the padded upper section can be removed easily; it is secured to the base with screws. Notice the way it is put together, and how the fabric is attached. For more about upholstery tools and techniques, see page 91.

MATERIALS AND TOOLS

The supplies will vary with the style and size of the stool. Look through the instructions to determine the needs for your project.

Fabric for cover

Polyester batting, if desired, for padding

Upholstery tacks and tack hammer

or

Heavy-duty stapler and staples

THE TOP COVER

1. Remove the old covering. Remove the staples, pulling out any broken staples with pliers.

2. Add extra padding, if desired. Cut batting the same as the cover (see step 3). Pull the batting tightly over the top and secure with a tack or staple at each side. Fold a pleat at each corner, pulling the material taut. Trim excess from inside the pleat to prevent a thick ridge, then tack the fabric under the frame. Tack around the frame, making sure the batting is very tight. Trim away excess around the edges.

   If the top fits into a recessed frame on the base, attach the padding so it won't interfere with the fit. Cut the padding to reach just to the point where the top fits into the frame.

Then make an under cover of thin fabric such as muslin to hold it in place. Cut and attach the muslin following the instructions for the outer cover, below.

3. Cut the outer fabric as a single piece to cover the top and sides, allowing ample margin to attach to the under side.

4. Attach the cover. Position on the top so any pattern is straight. Secure fabric on the underside with a tack at each side, pulling the fabric taut. At each corner, fold a pleat. Keep the fabric smooth and tight, and tack through the fold to the bottom. Continue tacking all around, keeping the fabric evenly taut across the top.

COVERING THE BASE

1. Cut batting as a strip to reach around the base, adding approximately 2 inches (5 cm) to the height.

2. Starting at a corner, tack to the bottom and top of the frame, keeping the fabric taut. At the end, trim so the edges abut rather than overlap. Trim off excess at the top and bottom.

3. Cut the fabric as for the padding, but allow approximately 4 inches (10 cm) overlap at the

ends, and allow additional margin at the top and bottom.

4. Start about an inch (2.5 cm) before a corner. Staple or tack the fabric tightly top and bottom, working around the stool. Form neat pleats at the corners. At the end, fold under the fabric edge so the fold will be at the corner.

5. If the legs are not recessed, carefully clip through the fabric margin to the edge of the base close to each side of the leg. Fold under the margin around the leg, trimming it slightly if necessary.

OPTIONS

Define the line where the top joins the base by adding welt trim made from matching fabric or with a contrasting pattern. Just tack it the along the lower edge of the top after the cover is in place. Instructions for making welt are on page 17.

CHECKED OTTOMAN

*N*eat tailored checks are a pleasant contrast to he chair's splash of flowers. The ottoman looks as if it were upholstered by a professional, but it is deceptively easy to achieve the same good-looking results in a short time.

Instructions for the chair slipcover are on page 73.

Welt is sewn into the seam around the top of the ottoman, with matching gimp to define the line between the top and base and to divide the base into two horizontal sections. This ottoman has a removable upper cushion and a padded base, a fairly common construction. There are all kinds of styles, though, and the best way to learn how your own piece is constructed—and how the new covering should be applied—is by taking off the old fabric.

MATERIALS AND TOOLS

The supplies you need will depend upon the style and size of the ottoman. Look through the instructions to determine the requirements for your project.

Fabric for cover

Purchased welt

Purchased gimp or braid trim to match welt.

Polyester batting, if desired, for padding

Cambric or dust cover cloth for bottom

Upholstery tacks and tack hammer

or

Heavy-duty stapler and staples

Fabric glue

THE TOP COVER

1. Remove the old covering. Pull out broken staples with pliers. Detach the top from the base.

2. Replenish the padding, if necessary. For the top, cut batting the same size as the cover (see step 3). Pull the batting tightly over the top and secure with a tack or staple on each side. Fold a pleat at each corner, pulling the material taut. Trim excess from inside the pleat to prevent a thick ridge, then tack the pleated fabric under the frame. Tack around the frame, making sure the batting is very tight. Trim excess from around the edges.

• For a top that fits into a recessed frame on the base, attach the padding so it won't interfere with the fit. Cut the padding to reach just to the point where the top fits into the frame. Then make an under cover of thin fabric such as muslin to hold it in place. Make the muslin cover just like the outer cover, below.

3. Cut the cover top to the dimensions of the top, adding seam allowance at all edges.

4. Cut or piece the edge strip for the upper section. For the total width of the strip, measure the perimeter at the upper edge and add seam allowances. For the height or length, to the height of the strip add seam allowance for the upper edge and approximately 2 inches (5 cm) at the lower edge.

5. Sew welt to the right side of the cover top. Detailed instructions for working with welt are on page 18.

6. Join the ends of the edge strip to make a circle. With the seam as one corner, mark the remaining corners.

7. Stitch the edge strip to the cover top with right sides together, stitching the top side along the previous stitching line. Clip the seam allowance as necessary at corners.

8. Place the cover wrong side out on the top to fit the corners. Pin a dart at each corner, as necessary, and pin the corner seam to adjust it. Carefully remove the cover and stitch the darts.

9. Replace the cover on the top and tack or staple to the underside around the edges. Start with a single tack at each side to position the fabric. Pull the fabric taut and even. Attach the corners next, then tack evenly all the way around.

10. Staple welt to the lower edge. Position it so the seam allowance is flat against the base of the top and the finished edge extends just slightly. Clip corners so welt will lie flat. Tuck in the ends.

COVERING THE BASE

1. Add new padding, if desired. Cut a piece slightly wider than the perimeter measurement of the base and with about 2 inches (5 cm) added at top and bottom. Wrap tightly around the base, beginning at one corner. Staple or tack top and under the base. For the join at the ends, abut the batting to avoid a ridge.

2. Cut fabric the same size as the batting, but with added allowance at the ends.

3. Start about an inch (2.5 cm) before a corner. Staple or tack the fabric tightly top and bottom, working around the base. At the end, fold under the fabric edge so the fold will be at the corner.

4. If the legs are not recessed, carefully clip through the fabric margin to the edge of the base close to each side of the leg. Fold under the margin around the leg, trimming it slightly if necessary.

5. To shape the base, tie a cord very tightly around at the point where the trim will be placed. Apply the gimp over the cord. Staple it invisibly, or use decorative tacks, or glue it with fabric glue.

6. Add a dust cover to the underside of the stool. Cut the fabric with 1-inch (2.5-cm) margins at all edges. Fold under the edges, and position with a tack at each side to hold the fabric, hen pull the fabric tightly and tack all the way around. Cut out a corner around each leg, leaving enough margin to turn under with the fold close to the leg. Clip from the edge to the fold as necessary so the fabric will lie flat.

OVERSTUFFED FOOTSTOOL

*B*old plaid fabric is an appropriate topping for this well-padded footstool. What appear to be insets of bias-cut fabric at the corners are actually just clever tucks in the single piece of fabric that forms the cover.

Reupholstering a stool like this one couldn't be easier. Even with the addition of extra padding, the job should be finished in an hour.

MATERIALS AND TOOLS

The supplies you need will depend upon the style and size of your footstool

Fabric for cover

Thick polyester batting for padding

Cambric or dust cover cloth for bottom

Upholstery tacks and tack hammer

or

Heavy-duty stapler and staples

COVERING THE STOOL

1. Remove the old cover. Pull out all of the staples.

2. Supplement the padding. Cut batting to extend over the top and sides of the stool, with approximately 2 inches (5 cm) margin all around.

3. Tack the batting to the underside. Pulling it taut, position it with one tack on each side. Fold a pleat at each side of each corner and fasten tightly. Then continue around the lower edge. Trim off the excess around the edges.

4. Cut cover fabric the size of the batting. Attach it in the same way, keeping the fabric straight and taut across the stool. Make a neat pleat at each side of each corner.

5. Attach the dust cover on the underside. Cut the fabric with 1-inch (2.5-cm) margins at all edges. Fold under the edges, and position with a tack at each side to hold the fabric, then pull the fabric tightly and tack all the way around. Cut out a corner around each leg, leaving enough margin to turn under with the fold close to the leg. Clip from the edge to the fold as necessary so the fabric will lie flat.

PILLOWS

There is nearly always enough fabric left for pillows after a major decorating project is finished. Each of these two is trimmed with fabric from the other. Instructions for making knife-edge pillows are on page 26.

8 ▪ Reupholstering a Chair

*U*pholstering involves little sewing. It's just a matter of fitting fabric panels over the padded frame, one at a time, and stapling them in place. The basic steps, shown in the photographs on the following pages, are the same for almost any piece of furniture.

An "average" chair consists of a wood frame, springs to support weight at the seat and sometimes the back, padding for comfort and shaping, then an outer fabric covering to hold it all together attractively.

The process of reupholstering a chair includes removing the fabric panels that make up the outer covering, removing at least some of the inner padding, checking that the frame is intact and the springs in working order, then supplementing the padding and putting the new cover fabric in place.

Generally, on a chair or couch, the inner areas—seat, back, and arms—are padded for comfort. The fabric panels covering these areas are usually secured tightly over the padding and attached to the outer frame, shaping the contours of the chair. The outer panels are often flat and have little padding. They are attached with tack strips of some kind so that the fabric edges can be turned under and secured invisibly over the stapled edges of the inner panels. Often welt, or piping, is used where the inner and outer panels meet to neaten the joins and provide a decorative element at the same time.

The photographs illustrate the process of recovering a wing chair. While the piece of furniture you plan to renovate may bear little resemblance to the model used here, the basic steps are similar for almost any piece of upholstered furniture. Look through the photographs to see how the steps shown here will relate to your chair or couch. Reupholstering is just a matter of careful observation and common sense.

Detailed information about upholstery materials and tools is given in Chapters 2 and 3. Look at Chapter 6, too; some of the slipcover details may work with your reupholstering project just as well.

PLANNING THE PROJECT

Sit down with a cup of coffee and a pad and pencil and do a thorough study of the chair you will re-cover. Make note of every construction detail. Draw diagrams to remind you, after the chair has been stripped, exactly how to put it back together. Polaroid snapshots can be helpful, too.

Where are the seams or joins? Do some, or all, the seams incorporate welt? If there is a skirt, how is it constructed and attached? Are there any features that would affect the fabric choice for the cover?

Look at the shape of the chair with regard to its padding. Are there any flattened or indented areas where padding should be added, such as on the tops of the arms and at the spot where the head rests against the inner back? Does the seat cushion look plump and inviting, or flattened and tired?

This stately wing chair is surely in need of re-covering. In order not to obscure the chair's graceful curves, the owner chose to reupholster rather than renovate with a less expensive, less fitted slipcover.

Before stripping the chair, the upholsterer made note of several construction details: There is welt around the lower edge and there is a separate welted panel at the top of the arm. There is also welt around the inner wing/inner arm seam, which is not always the case. The chair definitely needs more padding up the inner back and probably on all the inner areas.

TAKING MEASUREMENTS

Measure each covering section, or panel, and record the dimensions. Note the direction of the fabric grain on each piece. You will need this information to figure fabric requirements. Measure the total welt yardage (see page 17 for more about making welting). After the covering has been stripped, you can plan an accurate cutting layout and determine the amount of fabric you will need.

The drawings show the fabric sections that make up the chair's upholstery. The inner arm piece rolls over the top of the arm to join the side, or outer arm. The inner back joins the outer back in the same way. There is a separate panel on the front of the arm, and one between the inner and outer back at the shoulder.

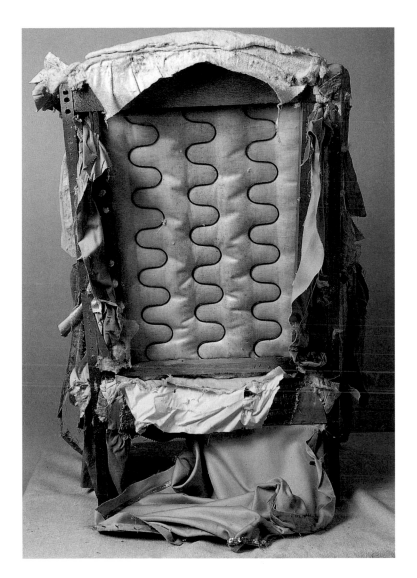

STRIPPING

Remove the old covering, one section at a time. Generally, the bottom dust cover is removed first, then all pieces that are secured to the bottom of the frame. The inner pieces are next; the deck usually is last. On the model chair the fabric panels will be taken off in this sequence:

> Dust cover
>
> Welt around the lower edge
>
> Outer back
>
> Outer arm
>
> Outer wing
>
> Inner back
>
> Inner wing
>
> Inner arm
>
> Platform, or deck,
>
> > and attached lower front panel

As each piece is removed, mark it as to its location. Note which pieces are sewn together. Also note how each piece was attached, whether stapled or held in place with a tacking strip or flexible metal strip. Save the pieces to plan the cutting layout for the new fabric and to use as patterns for fitted pieces.

The dust covering and welt were removed from the bottom of the chair, then the outer back panel. Two additional layers of covering were discovered underneath, with padding added over each. Since additional padding was needed under this covering, it was best to remove all the old layers and work from the frame.

The green fabric edges visible at the between the vertical sections of the frame on each side are the inner back pull-through margins. These had been stapled to the frame on the outer back. Below the springs is the pull-through at the lower edge of the inner back. Since the pull-through is not visible when the job is finished, waste fabric can be used in those areas in the interest of fabric economy.

The upper edge of the outer back was attached with a flexible metal tack strip to accommodate the curve at the top of the chair.

Save the old fabric pieces. They can be used to plan the cutting layout for the new covering, then as rough patterns for the new pieces. If new padding is added, be sure to try each piece for fit before using it as a pattern, and make any necessary adjustments.

Pull out the old staples—all of them. Use pliers to remove broken staples, or tap them well into the wood with a tacking hammer so no sharp ends protrude.

Determine the condition of the padding. It may be that only a small amount of new padding is needed to fill in areas where the material has compacted, such as at the center of the inner back and on the deck. If considerable work is needed, remove the padding. Save it for reuse if it is in good condition and free of dust and mildew.

Repair loose sections of the frame. Replace burlap and webbing that is torn or stretched out of shape (working with webbing is described on page 92). Re-tie or replace springs if necessary.

Plan to replace foam cushions that have developed hard spots or indentations, or that have begun to disintegrate. A layer of polyester batting can be added to a foam cushion that simply needs a little additional loft.

FABRIC AND MATERIALS

After the chair has been stripped you can figure the amount of fabric you will need for the new cover. If you have not chosen a fabric, plan for fabric 54 inches (137 cm) wide, the most common width for upholstery fabrics.

Fabric panels normally are cut with their vertical orientation on the lengthwise grain, with the pattern direction as indicated by the arrows in the diagrams. In other words, a pattern should read upward on the most visible areas: the inner and outer back, outer arms, and front. This also means that nap direction, as on velvet or corduroy, will be just the opposite—it will be smooth in the downward direction.

On a couch, you can save considerable yardage—and time—if the fabric can be "railroaded," or cut with the lengthwise grain running the width of the couch. This way, the outer and inner back pieces can each be cut as a single piece. The technique won't work with directional patterns or napped fabrics. Some fabrics are made with railroading in mind, for example with stripes woven across the width instead of lengthwise.

Draw a layout diagram to calculate the fabric yardage. Position the large pieces on the diagram first, then fill in with smaller ones. Be sure to lay out the pieces with the correct fabric grain orientation.

Add pull-through allowances and seam allowances according to the pieces that were removed. Remember, though, that fabric may have been trimmed away from some edges after they were stapled, so be generous with these allowances.

If the covering fabric is in short supply or extraordinarily expensive, waste fabric can be used for the pull-through margins. In this case, cut the good cover fabric slightly longer and wider than the visible area and tuck-in. Cut waste pieces on the same fabric grain. Overlap edges for a flat seam, and zigzag the two fabrics together.

Make a list of other materials and supplies you will need. Note sizes of the deck section and bottom dust covering. List padding, cushion material, tack strips, welt cord, and threads too.

REPLENISH THE PADDING

Replace or supplement the padding as necessary. Pad the platform first, replace the cover for that section, then add padding to the inner arms and back. Padding of the outer panels can be done as those panels are put in place.

Use the original work as a guide as to the kind of padding material and the amount used in each area. Often cotton felt or batting makes up the under layer and polyester batting the final layer under the cover fabric.

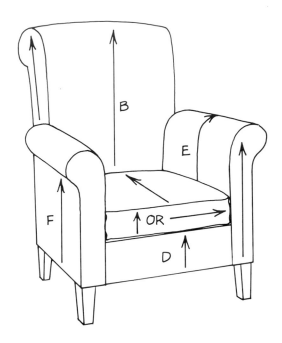

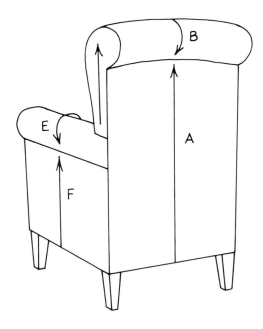

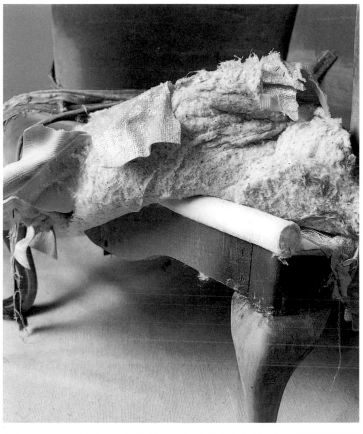

The platform/front panel was detached at the bottom of the chair to check the condition of the springs and deck padding. This chair has a firm front edge with a strip of edge roll to define the front and keep the cushion in place. Note that the under layers of padding are cut just to the edge roll, with the top layers extending over the edge.

The springs were tight and only one additional layer of cotton batting is needed. The old covering will be fastened back in place; the new platform will be applied over it.

Work each section so it is evenly taut, and staple it to the frame, following the pattern of the original materials. Make neat tucks at corners. Trim at exposed edges. With the mallet, gently pound the padding across edges so that lines and contours are smooth and even.

Padding can be used to create contours, for example at the lower part of the inner back. Build up the area by adding smaller pieces of padding as the inner layers, so that the outer padding will cover the entire section and give a smooth finished appearance.

The new padding on the inner sections of this wing chair follows the lines of the covering. The upper edges of the outer panels will be placed just above the rows of staples securing the padding.

A fiberboard panel sometimes is used to cover the hollow in the wing frame.

When padding is added to the inner back and inner arms, be sure to check that the cushion will fit. Add padding to the cushion top if it's needed.

THE MUSLIN COVER

An inner muslin cover is a feature of some of the most costly professional jobs. There are advantages to adding this extra step to a home reupholstery job, too. For a novice, it affords practice with cutting and fitting. The fit can be perfected before expensive fabric is cut. With the muslin cover in place, unevenness in the padding will be visible and can be corrected before the final covering is applied.

To make a muslin cover, cut fabric and apply it according to the steps for applying the final cover, omitting the welt. Use the mallet and stuffing regulator to smooth out the padding.

REUPHOLSTERING THE CHAIR

Block out the new cover pieces on the chair. Working on the chair, cut the cover panels roughly to size, allowing plenty of margin. Use the old pieces for guides as to seam allowance and pull-through margin, but do the actual fitting on the chair to adjust for new padding and for the old fabric having stretched out of shape. Cut each panel to final size as it is attached to the chair.

For the chair in the photos that follow, panels were applied in this sequence:

> Platform/front
>
> Inner arm
>
> Inner wing
>
> Inner back
>
> Outer wing
>
> Outer arm
>
> Outer back
>
> Lower welt and dust cover

1. Welt Strips

Cut fabric strips for welt. Make the welt, sewing an extra ½ yard (.5 m) or more of welt so there will be enough to avoid placing seams in awkward places. Detailed instructions for making welt are on page 17.

2. Platform and Front

Sew the platform and front sections together, stitching just between the corner darts. With the piece wrong side out on the chair, pin the corner darts. Turn it right side out and adjust for fit. Stitch and trim the darts.

Put the cover in place so the corners are snug. Sew the platform cover in place across the deck.

Fold the platform cloth forward along the seamline. Starting at the dart, take a stitch through the padding and burlap below it if possible. Pull the needle through, leaving a long thread tail. Take the second stitch and knot the thread securely to the tail.

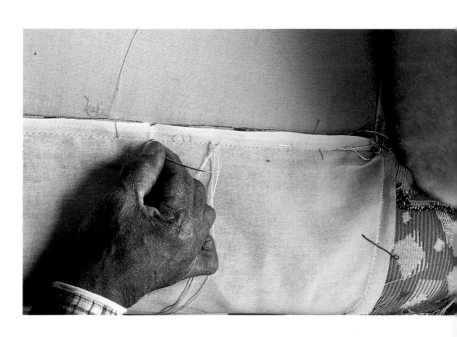

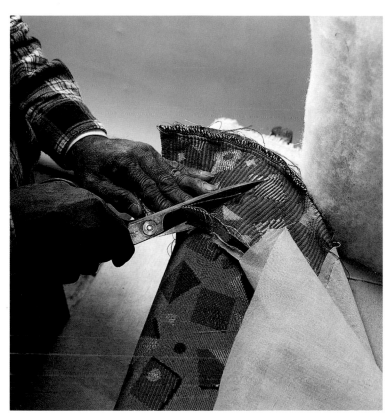

Clip the corners to fit the platform and front.

Fold the sides inward, the folds against the inner arms. Make a diagonal clip from the corner of each margin to within about 3 inches (7 cm) of the arm as shown.

Pull the front section of the margin tightly down in front of the arm; pull the side extension through to the outside of the frame.

Secure the lower front edge with a few temporary staples on the underside of the frame. Make diagonal clips at the back corners as was done at the front, and pull through the frame at the back and sides.

The platform/front section is fitted at the front corners and will be tightened up when the inner arm cover is in place.

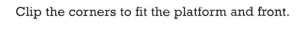

3. The Inner Arm

This chair is somewhat unusual in that the top of the arm is covered with a separate fabric panel rather than being an extension of the inner arm panel. The inner arm cover is stapled to the outer frame at the placement point for the outer arm panel. The lower edge is pulled through the frame and stapled in place.

With the inner arm in place, the front corner can be tightened. The inner arm panel is pulled very tightly downward at the front to form a pleat over the front panel, then stapled under the frame.

The upper arm panel has been sewn to the inner arm, then the two handled as a single inner arm panel. Welt is incorporated into the seam and sufficient length is left to attach at the outer arm join as shown in the next photo.

The vertical and horizontal rows of staples attaching the inner arm cover to the outer frame indicate placement for the outer arm panel. The lower edges of the inner arm padding and cover have been pulled through the frame.

4. The Inner Wing

The inner wing cover is pulled through the frame along the back. Around the outer edge of the wing it is stapled to the frame. The staple line is far enough from the edge that it won't interfere with the tack strip that will be used to attach the outer wing panel. The lower edge can simply be turned under where it overlaps the inner arm or, as with this chair, be trimmed with welt.

Welt was sewn to the lower edge of the inner wing section. As the fabric is pulled around the outer edge of the wing, fabric is clipped to the staple line to assure a smooth fit.

5. The Inner Back

Tuck the sides of the inner back in at the back/inner wing crevice. At the top, pull the fabric over the frame and staple it in place temporarily.

Waste fabric was used for the pull-through at the sides of the inner back. Excess fabric around the inner wing section will be trimmed off.

At the lower edge, clip the fabric parallel to the bottom of the panel, cutting inward from the edge to a point several inches below the visible lower edge of the back. Keep these lower sections free and pull the center portion of the lower back through the back of the frame.

The sides and lower edge of the inner back were pulled through the frame. The tab visible on the platform is the section below the point where the clip was made at the side.

On the outer arm, a slit is cut in the inner arm pull-through. The inner back tab is pulled taut through the slit and stapled to the frame. This helps hold the inner back fabric securely.

6. The Outer Wing

Staple welt around the outer wing, clipping
or notching the seam allowance as necessary. The fine points of welt application
are described on page 18.

*On the outer wing, excess padding
and fabric were trimmed at the
inner wing staple line before welt
was attached.*

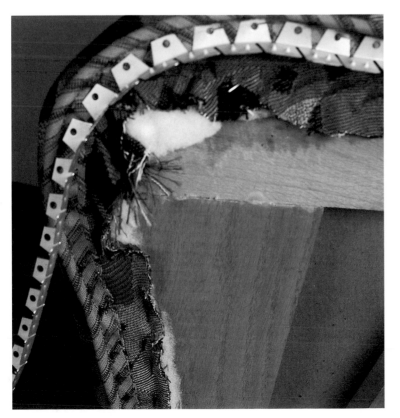

With flexible metal tack strip the curved
outer edge of the outer wing panel can be
attached smoothly and neatly. The fabric
must be trimmed so that the margin around
the placement line is equal in width to
the outer half of the strip (with tacks).
Mark the placement line on the panel
with chalk, then trim carefully.

*The edge of the flexible strip that
will be stapled to the frame is
positioned just under the welt.*

The strip is stapled with precision; one end of the staple goes into the hole in a section of the strip, the other directly into the wood.

A single thickness of polyester batting pads the wing.

Batting is trimmed to the fold of the tack strip.

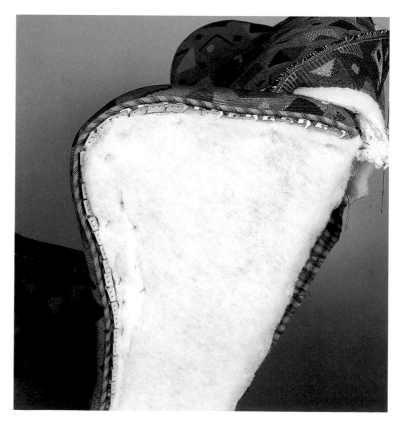

Press the panel margin onto the tack half of the strip with the fabric outer edge in the center groove of the strip. Press the edge of the strip to fold it in half and enclose the fabric edge.

A stuffing regulator helps press the panel edge firmly in place.

Tap gently with the mallet to press the tacks into the wood.

Now the upper edge of the inner back can be stapled permanently along the outer frame.

Pliers make it easier to pull a panel tightly enough to achieve a taut fit.

7. The Outer Arm

The outer arm is attached without padding or batting.

Chalk-mark the finished edges on the outer arm panel. Position the panel with the upper chalked line against the placement line on the chair. Staple close to the line.

The free end of the upper arm panel welting is stapled across to the lower edge of the outer wing panel.

The upper edge of the panel can be attached with just enough staples to hold it in place. A tack strip will be placed over it.

Cut fiber tacking strip to reach a strip's width short of the vertical placement line for the panel at the inner arm roll and back corner. The upper edge of the strip is at the placement line.

The strip is stapled close to its upper edge, and the panel pulled down over it.

For the front vertical edge, cut a length of tack strip that extends from just above the lower edge of the chair to the bottom of the horizontal strip. Press fabric margin onto the tacks, aligning the inner edge of the strip with the chalked placement line on the fabric.

Fold the fabric margin and strip to the wrong side of the panel. Press the strip in place on the chair.

Press the tacked edge of the panel in place by hand to make sure the tacks go into the wood without bending. Then tap along the strip with the mallet.

Since the fiber strips did not extend to the upper front corner, it must be secured somehow. Use a brad to hold it invisibly, or use a decorative tack.

The back and lower edges of the panel are stapled to the frame.

8. The Outer Back

The outer back panel is attached in the same way as the outer arm. Flexible metal tack strip was used across the top to accommodate the curve. Fiber tacking strip was used for the first vertical edge and tack strip for the second. The lower edge was stapled to the frame.

Just the right combination of fabric can produce some extraordinary effects. The same fabric was used for the back and the welt, but because the welt was cut on the bias the two appear to be different, although related, patterns.

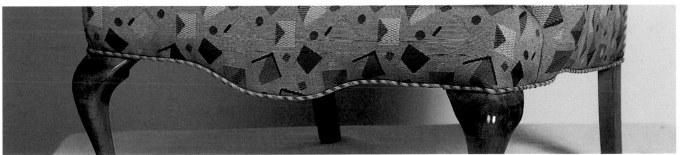

9. Finishing the Lower Edges

Starting at the back close to a corner, attach the welt and turn under the panels around the legs. Fasten the end of the welt to the frame, then turn under the fabric around one leg, easing the welt seam allowance under the fabric. Clip through the welt seam allowance at each side of the corner. Staple the welt to the frame along the straight side and work around the other legs and sides in the same way.

10. The Dust Cover

Cut the dust cover fabric with generous margins. Folding under the edges, staple the center of each side to the frame, pulling the cover taut. Continue stapling the sides almost to the legs.

Cut away the fabric around the legs, again leaving a margin. Turn under the edges, keeping the fold close to the leg. Clip from the edge to the fold as necessary so the fabric will lie flat at the foldline.

On this chair the front edge of the dust cover was extended to reach the lower edge of the chair's decorative front panel.

The procedure for re-covering a couch is almost the same as for a chair, with a few differences due to the extra width. It is often necessary to piece widths of fabric across the front and on the inner and outer back. Details are illustrated in the chapter on slipcovers, beginning on page 56. If the fabric can be railroaded—applied with the lengthwise grain of the fabric across the width of the back—piecing may not be necessary except at the lower front.

ADDING A SKIRT

Many upholstered pieces have skirts around the lower edge; on others, one can be added without detracting from the appearance of the piece. Construct the new skirt using the existing skirt as a guide, or refer to the instructions in the slipcover chapter, page 70.

A skirt for an upholstred piece usually should be lined, rather than doubled, because of the relatively thicker fabric. Use buckram or stiff interfacing so the skirt will hold its shape.

Prepare welt equal in length to the finished width of the skirt. Sew the welt to the right side of the skirt, matching seamlines.

Mark the upper placement line of the skirt on the chair.

Position the skirt wrong side up on the chair with the welt along the placement line and the lower edge upward as shown. Place lengths of fiber tacking strip over the seam allowance and staple in place.

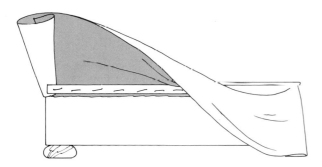

9 ▪ Upholstery Projects

*R*eupholstery differs from slipcover making in that the new cover fabric is attached to the furniture, more or less permanently. Except for making the welt, there is little sewing involved. Repholstering also can include structural improvements, such as replacing or replenishing padding under the cover.

There is a permanence about reupholstering. A new slipcover might be intended to last for just a short time, or be used as a temporary measure until a piece can be reupholstered. Reupholstering projects are begun on the premise that the work will last the life of the furniture—or of the upholsterer.

The projects in this chapter require some time and patience. It is possible that none of the furniture shown in the photographs is identical to the piece that you would like to re-cover. Each project features a few unusual details, and some of the procedures are likely to apply to your own project. If there is an aspect to your project that has you bewildered, look through the instructions in this chapter and the previous one; you will probably find the information you need.

A ROOM FOR COMFORT

*S*ubdued shades create an atmosphere that is restful and appealing.
The couch and its cushions all are covered in medium-weight cotton
fabric, simple and unassuming, and a pleasure to sew.

THE COUCH

This couch is upholstered according to the instructions illustrated in Chapter 8. The fabric is lighter weight than traditional upholstery material, so requires a little extra attention to even distribution of padding materials under the covering. This is a case where it would be beneficial, and perhaps save time in the long run, to attach an under cover of muslin before applying the outer cover fabric.

The use of a solid-colored, even-weave material allowed for railroading the fabric across the inner and outer back and the front. This technique can save time, as it means piecing seams aren't needed in these areas.

Separate panels cover the fronts of the arms. They are applied after the inner arm fabric is pleated tightly and stapled around the arm front. The front panel is made of a piece of fiberboard cut to shape, with padding and fabric stapled over it. Welt usually is added around the outer edge. Pieces of tack strip are stapled to the back of the panel, tack side up, to fasten the panel in place at the arm front.

CUSHIONS AND PILLOWS

Firm seat cushions and softer back cushions are made in the traditional box style, edged with welt. The accent pillows are the knife-edge variety, also with welted seams. Instructions for making both pillow styles begin on page 26.

PATCHWORK UPHOLSTERY

The unusual lines of this chair call for out-of-the ordinary upholstery. Crayon-bright prints—less than two yards of any one pattern—combine for an effect that certainly fills the bill.

The chair's cotton covering fabrics are lighter weight material than is normally used for upholstery. It is important to make sure the padding is smooth and evenly distributed when the covering is applied. For an inexperienced upholsterer, it would be a good idea to make an inner muslin cover before putting the final covering in place. This allows you to see the final shape of the chair, and to even out the padding with a stuffing regulator.

Follow the upholstery procedures illustrated in Chapter 8. This chair has several features that indicate a slightly different approach.

1. The back is a separate cushion that rests against an exposed wooden frame. It is an ordinary box cushion, made according to the instructions on page 27. Since it is meant to give firm support, the inner cushion is foam instead of the softer fillings often used for back cushions with chairs that have upholstered backs.

2. Since there is not a separate seat cushion, the front/deck seam is at the front edge. Welt, to match that on the back cushion, defines the front seamline.

3. A single panel covers the well-padded inner and outer arm, with a front and back panel—also well padded—to cover the ends of each arm. The front and back panels are made of fiberboard, cut and padded to shape. Fabric is stapled over the edges. Pieces of tack strip are stapled to the back of the panel, tack side up, to fasten the panel in place on the arm.

UPHOLSTERED BOXES

Scraps left from the larger upholstery project can provide unusual accent pieces and always-welcome storage space at the same time. Sturdy fiberboard boxes are available at crafts supply stores, ready to cover.

Sturdy cardboard box with lid

Fabric for outer covering

Fabric for lining

White glue and brush

Acrylic spray, if desired

INSTRUCTIONS

1. Cut outer fabric for the box. Cut one piece as wide as the box perimeter plus 1 inch (2.5 cm), and in length, the height of the box plus 2 inches (5 cm). Cut a piece for the bottom that is approximately ½ inch (1 cm) smaller on each side. For the lid, cut fabric the size of the lid plus three times the lid depth added to each side.

2. For the lining, cut the main piece and bottom section the same as for the outer fabric. For the lid, cut the piece slightly smaller than the lid inner dimensions.

3. To apply the fabric to the box, spread glue over a small area at a time. Allow it to dry slightly, then apply a section of fabric and smooth it in place. Take care not to stretch the damp fabric. Start ½ inch (1 cm) before a corner of the box. Glue the edge of the fabric at this point, allowing equal fabric margins top and bottom. Continue around the box, folding under the end so the fold is at the corner.

4. Glue the upper edges tightly to the inside, folding neat pleats at the corners. Glue the lower edges to the underside of the box, mitering the corners. Glue the bottom section in place.

5. For the lining, press one long edge approximately ¾ inch (2 cm) to the wrong side. Glue it around the inside of the box with the fold near the upper edge. Glue the bottom section in place.

6. For the lid, glue the piece, centered, to the top of the lid. Glue fabric tightly over the edges, clipping out excess if necessary at the corners so there is no fabric thickness to interfere with the fit of the lid. Glue the lining square in place.

7. When the box is completely dry, coat with acrylic spray, if desired, to protect the fabric. Test the spray first with a scrap.

UPHOLSTERED TABLE

*A*n upholstered table? Why not? It is easier, and certainly much quicker, to cover an old wooden table with fabric than to strip and refinish it. And the results are most impressive.

The table looks nothing like the wing chair used to illustrate basic upholstery techniques in Chapter 8, but the same materials and procedures are used. Choose a sturdy fabric, such as medium to heavy cotton or cotton blend, for the best results.

MATERIALS

Fabric for the table cover

Contrast or matching fabric for welt

Welt cord

Polyester batting, ⅜ to ½ inch
    (1 to 1.3 cm) thick

Fiber tack strips equal in length to the
    tabletop perimeter measurement
    plus four times the leg length

Stapler and staples

INSTRUCTIONS

1. Make welt equal in length to the perimeter of the table top plus approximately 2 inches (5 cm). Detailed instructions for making and attaching welt are on page 17.

2. Staple batting to the table top, edges, and legs. For the top, cut a piece large enough to extend well under the sides all around. Cut away excess at the corners to avoid overlapping.

3. For the legs, cut pieces of batting long enough to meet, or slightly overlap the top piece and to extend under the bottoms of the legs. Allow for slight overlap in the width. Staple in place, positioning the overlap on an inner side of each leg.

4. For the table top, cut fabric to the tabletop dimensions plus 1 inch (2.5 cm) margin at each edge.

5. Cut fabric for the edges. In width, cut each piece approximately 2 inches (5 cm) wider than the distance between the legs. In length, cut with a 2-inch (5-cm) margin at the top and lower edge.

6. Cut fabric for the legs. Cut each piece 4 inches (10 cm) longer than the leg length measured from the table top, and 2 inches (5 cm) wider than the circumference of the leg at the widest point.

7. Attach the edge strips. Staple the upper edge across the table top, keeping the line of staples approximately 1 inch from the edge. Pull the fabric taut and staple to the underside. At the legs, make a horizontal cut, even with the bottom of the table edge, from the fabric edge to the inner

edge of the leg. Pull the lower half of this piece to the underside of the table. Fold under to just meet the leg, trimming as necessary, and staple in place. On the outer edge of the table, leave the piece extending onto the leg. Attach the remaining edge strips in the same way.

8. Cover the legs. Align the vertical center of each strip along the outer corner of the leg. Staple the upper edge over the table top and the lower edge to the bottom of the leg, using just one staple at each point to hold the piece in place.

9. Wrap one long edge of the fabric around the leg, keeping the fabric straight at the outer corner. Staple close to the fabric edge. Where the leg meets the edge of the table, make a horizontal clip, even with the lower edge of the table, from the fabric edge to the inner corner of the leg. Pull the lower half of this piece around to the inside of the leg. Turn under the top edge, trimming as necessary, and staple. Fold under the margin up the remainder of the outside of the leg and staple to the top. Clip away fabric at the top corner to reduce the bulk.

10. For the remaining long edge of the leg, pull the fabric tightly around the leg. Fold under the fabric margin so the fold is even with the inner corner of the leg. Finger press the crease. Work the leg/edge corner as for the other side.

11. Cut a length of tack strip equal to the leg length from the floor to folded upper edge of the fabric. Place the strip in the fold of the fabric, tacks through the seam allowance. Tap firmly into the leg up the inner corner.

12. Now staple the ends securely to the table top and under the leg. Finish the other legs in the same way.

13. Beginning at one corner, staple the welt around the perimeter of the top. Position so the finished edge of the welt extends slightly beyond the table edge. Staple close to the unfinished edge of the welt. Cut away notches at the corners to avoid overlap.

14. Fold under and crease the margin around the table top section, clipping diagonally almost to the fold at each corner.

15. Cut a length of tack strip for each side of the top. Each should be the length of the side less twice the width of the strip.

16. Working one side of the table at a time, place a strip in the crease of the fabric as for the legs, centering the strip along the length to leave the margin at each end. Tap the edge in place, the fold up close to the welt.

17. Work an adjacent side next, and continue around the table.

SHADES OF RED

*D*espite the mix of bold patterns and strong colors, this room has a warm, restful feel. A blend of upholstered pieces, all curves and cushions, implies comfort and hospitality.

Most of the upholstery techniques used for re-covering these pieces are illustrated in Chapter 8. Each one has an unusual detail or two worth mentioning.

Gingham-Covered Wing Chair

Its gaily checked cover is somewhat anachronistic, yet it enhances the chair's handsome lines. When the fabric has a geometric pattern like this, the pieces must be attached with absolute precision; waviness along the grainlines would produce a dizzying effect.

The procedure for re-covering this chair is almost identical to that illustrated for the wing chair in Chapter 8. There are just a few differences.

1. The outer wings have extra padding above the line of the outer side panel. This look is accomplished by adding small pieces of padding for thickness in certain areas, then adding padding over the entire panel.

2. The inner arm rolls to the outside, the panel ending at the upper line of the outer arm panel.

3. Separate panels are used at the arm front areas. They are applied after the inner arm fabric is stapled around the arm front. The front panel is made of a piece of fiberboard cut to shape, with padding and fabric stapled over it. Welt usually is stapled around the outer edge. Pieces of tack strip are stapled to the back of the panel, tack side up, to fasten the piece to the front of the arm. These panels sport fabric-covered buttons that were sewn to the panels before the panels were secured in place.

Ivory-Colored Love Seat

Instead of a panel at the arm front, the inner arm rolls to the outside at both front and side. It is shaped to fit with neat pleats that converge at the upper corner of the outer arm panel.

The seat cushion is covered in an unusual fashion. A single piece of fabric covers the top, front edge, and bottom of the cushion, the edges meeting at the zipper seam along the back. Insets at the cushion's ends are curved to match the roll of the edges.

Red and White Plaid Stool

The covering style used for the stool at the end of the couch is so simple that it can be applied in an hour.

Materials

Fabric for the cover

Dust cover fabric, if desired

Fiber tack strips, enough length to equal the perimeter measurement at the base of the stool

Staple gun and staples

Instructions

1. Cut fabric for the top. The piece should be large enough to extend approximately 2 inches (5 cm) to the underside all around.

2. Staple the fabric tightly along the bottom of the stool. Staple the center of each edge first.

3. At each corner, make a pleat. Fold it so that it lies vertically to one side of the actual corner. Staple securely.

4. At each leg, clip the fabric margin from the edge just to the lower edge of the stool, making a cut right at each leg join. Staple up to the clip on each side of the leg.

5. Around the leg, trim away the fabric margin so the edge is even with that of the old upholstery.

6. Cut a strip of fabric approximately 2 inches (5 cm) longer than the perimeter measurement at the lower edge of the stool. In width, cut it not quite three times the width of the tack strip.

7. Cut a length of tack strip for each side of the stool, each 3 inches (8 cm) shorter than the length of the side on which it will be used.

8. Fold the fabric tightly around one tack strip length, leaving 2 inches (5 cm) at the fabric end and pressing the two fabric edges onto the tacks.

9. Beginning at a corner on the appropriate side, press the strip onto the stool. The beginning of

the tack strip should be placed approximately 1½ inches (4 cm) from the corner. There should not be tack strip under the fabric at any of the corner positions. At the end, fold the unfinished fabric end tightly over the tack strip and place it so that it covers the beginning.

10. To neaten the underside of the piece, add a dust cover (see page 124).

RED PLAID CHAIR

The arrangement of the pattern on each panel is a good example of excellent planning. Notice how the strongest element of the pattern is perfectly centered up the front. It is matched along the seat depth too—a feat made easier by the absence of a separate seat cushion.

The second most visible areas—the outer arms—exhibit perfection in balance and stripes that line up precisely at the inner arm/outer arm join.

The upholstering itself is straightforward. The techniques shown in Chapter 8 apply equally well here; there are just a few different features on this chair.

1. The wing, of course, is absent. But the inner back/inner arm join on this chair is handled in exactly the same manner as the inner wing/inner arm join on the Chapter 8 model.

2. The plaid chair has no upper arm panel. That piece was secured under the outer arm panel just as the inner arm joins the outer arm panel on this chair.

3. Like the gingham-covered wing chair, this one has separate front arm panels. They are made up in the same way. These, however, are held in place by decorative tacks.

An Array of Plaids

*S*trong plaids suit the larger proportions of this couch and chair, while a compatible pattern on a slightly smaller scale works better for the child's chair and footstool.

Instructions for upholstering the footstool are on page 103.

The Couch and Chair

Smooth pattern matching is essential with fabrics like these. Normally, the seat cushion covers would be cut with the pattern corresponding to that of the inner back and front. But to alleviate the regularity of the stripe pattern that would have resulted, this upholsterer alternated the stripe colors on the cushion covers.

These pieces can be upholstered according to the procedures illustrated in Chapter 8, with just a few differences.

1. There is a separate shoulder panel at each side of the back. It is attached over a piece of batting that has been cut to fit and stapled in place. The outer panel is fitted using flexible metal tack strip as shown for the outer wing panel on page 118.

2. Separate panels cover the fronts of the arms. The inner and outer arms are covered first. The front panel is cut to shape from fiberboard, padded lightly, then covered with fabric that is stapled to the back. A strip of welt is stapled around the edge. Pieces of tack strip are stapled to the back of the panel, tack side up, to fasten the panel in place at the arm front.

3. With the heavy padding on the inner back, separate back cushions aren't used. Knife-edge pillows, covered to match, provide a casual accent. Instructions for making the pillows are on page 26.

Child's Chair

The seat of this graceful little chair fits into a recessed frame and is easy to remove for re-covering. On page 91 are complete instructions for supplementing the padding and reupholstering the seat. Welt is tacked around the edge after the covering is in place.

The upholstered back is in two sections. The outer back, edged with welt, is attached with tack strips to the frame. With the outer back removed, the inner back can be taken out of the recessed frame. The outer back is handled in the same way as the outer wing panel of the chair used to illustrate basic upholstery techniques, page 118.

A Summer Attitude

Wicker has a way of filling a room with the spirit of summer, no matter how dreary the weather outside. With their sleek upholstery, these handsome pieces are at home in all but the most formal of rooms.

The covering of these pieces combines slipcover-making techniques and those of upholstery. Careful fitting produces the smoothly finished look.

For the inner back and arms, layers of padding are graduated in size from the frame outward to create the shape. Firmer cotton batting is used for the under layers, with a final layer of polyester batting that extends to the upper edge and smooths out the curve.

Welt is stapled in place along the upper edges and outer edges of the arms. The fabric panels are stapled at the bottom, and at the top are fitted in place with tack strips, or with flexible metal tack strips for the curves. These techniques are illustrated on pages 117 and 120.

The seats are loose cushions with very fitted covers. A foam base is wrapped tightly with polyester batting to round the edges. The cover seams are sewn with the back left open. With the cover in place, the back is sewn closed with a curved upholstery needle.

Index

Arm front
in slipcovers, 54, 81, 87
upholstered, 129, 130

Arm, inner
in slipcovers, 54, 61-62, 64, 65
upholstered, 114, 130

Arm, outer
in slipcovers, 54, 63
upholstered, 106, 120-122

Back, inner
in slipcovers, 54, 58-59, 61, 65
upholstered 106, 115

Back, outer
in slipcovers, 54, 57
upholstered, 106, 108, 123

Batting, 15, 16, 93

Blocking out
slipcovers, 57-65
upholstery panels, 112

Bottom cloth, 15. *See also* Dust cover

Bottom finishing
of slipcovers, 71
of upholstery, 123-124

Boxes, upholstered, 130

Break-away, 58, 70

Burlap, 92

Buttonholes, bound, 77

Cambric, 15

Chair, child's, upholstering 138

Chairs
reupholstery for 112, 129, 134, 135, 136, 138
straight, slipcovers for, 36-39, 42-44, 47, 48-49, 51
straight, reupolstery for, 91-93, 95, 96, 97
upholstered, slipcovers for, 67-69, 73, 74, 78, 81, 85, 87, 89

Coir fiber, 16, 93

Cord, spring tying, 16

Cord, welt, 15

Cotton felt, 15, 16

Couches
slipcovers for, 53-68, 79, 81, 83
upholstery for, 129, 134, 136

Cushioned camp stool, 31

Cushion-topped ottoman, 45, 83

Cushions and pillows, 25-32. *See also* Pillows
fillings for, 25
measuring for covers, 57

Cushions, box 27-28, 31, 57

Darts and tucks, in slipcovers, 61, 62, 69

Deck
in slipcovers, 54, 59
upholstering, 112, 113

Decking fabric, 15

Down, 25, 92

Dressing table cover, 44

Drop-in seat, reupholstering, 91-93, 94, 95,

Dust cover, 15, 93, 124

Edge roll, 15

Fabric, 11-15
decorator, 13
patterned, 13
preshrinking, 15, 55
for slipcovers and upholstery, 14-15, 53, 91-92
striped, working with, 13, 67-69
weaves of, 12
yardage requirements for slipcovers, 54, 55
yardage requirements for upholstery, 106, 109, 110

Fabric grain, 13-14
on slipcovers, 54
of upholstery, 110

Feathers, 25, 92

Foam, 25, 109

Footstool, pillow-topped, 35

Footstools and ottomans
slipcovers for, 34-36, 45, 83
upholstering, 99, 100, 103, 134

Front panel
of slipcover, 54, 60-61
of upholstery, 112, 113

Gussets, in slipcovers, 87

Kapok, 25

Mallets, 23, 119

Muslin covers, 93, 112

Needlepoint upholstery, 98

Needles
    hand sewing, 23
    sewing machine, 21-22

Ottoman, cushion-topped, 83

Ottomans. *See* Footstools and ottomans

Padding
    replacement of, 91-93, 105, 108, 110-111
    for upholstered furniture, 16

Pillow
    knife-edge 26-27, 83, 103
    soft box, 28-29
    tied, 83

Pillows. *See also* Cushions

Piping. *See* Welt

Platform. *See* Deck

Platform cloth, 15, 112

Pleats, box, at slipcover back, 40-41

Preshrinking fabrics, 15, 55

Presser feet, 22

Pull-through margin, 107, 110, 112, 113, 114, 116

Railroading, 55, 57, 59, 109, 124

Seat, drop-in, 91-93

Skirts, 54, 56, 59, 60, 61, 66-67, 70, 125
    box pleated, 85

Slipcover
    with apron, 89
    with box-pleated skirt, 85
    for captain's chair, 51
    draped linen, 47
    with buttoned back, 74

Slipcovers, straight chair,
    designs for, 36-39, 42-44, 47, 48-49, 51
    measuring for, 48-49

Slipcovers, upholstered chair or couch
    cutting and fitting, 53-68
    designs for, 67-69, 73, 74, 78, 79, 81, 83, 85, 87, 89
    fabric requirements for, 54, 55

Slipcovers, footstool and ottoman, 34-36, 45, 83

Spring front edge, 58, 61

Staple remover 23

Staplers and staples, 23, 91-92, 108

Stripping upholstered furniture, 91-92, 106-107

Stuffing regulator, 23, 93, 119

Table, upholstered, 131

Tack strip, 17, 108, 117-118, 121, 122
    flexible metal, 117-118

Tacking strip, 17, 121

Tacks, upholstery, 16, 91, 92

Ties, for slipcovers, 40, 85

Tools, upholstery, 22-23

Trims, decorative, 13, 100

Tuck-in allowance, 54, 58, 59, 61, 65

Tucks. *See* Darts and tucks

Webbing stretcher, 23, 92

Webbing, 15, 92

Welt 13, 17-19, 70, 95, 107, 112, 123

Wicker furniture, upholstering, 138

Wing
    on slipcover, 62, 65
    upholstering, 115, 117-119

Wing chair, reupholstering, 109, 112-125

Zippers, 16
    installation in cushions, 26, 27, 28, 29
    installation in slipcovers, 53, 71